Museums and Nationalism in Croatia, Hungary, and Turkey

Museums and Nationalism in Croatia, Hungary, and Turkey draws attention to museums as political productions of the nation-state and shows how they can be shaped by the political forces that rule a country.

Drawing on case studies and interviews from Croatia, Hungary, and Turkey, the book investigates how the past has been exploited to serve the interests of nationalism in the 21st century, and how museums themselves are exploited to serve nationalist ideologies. Posocco argues that, in a world of nation-states where nationalism is the dominant ideology, all museums are national museums, even when they aren't. In this perspective, they can (and do, in the case studies under analysis in this book) become the cultural offshoots of political wars, places where the national past is contested, rewritten, and sometimes even created from scratch, and finally exhibited. Paying particular attention to the decision-making and economic aspects of the museum, the book also examines the micro-sociological and political aspects, which will be the foundation for further reflections on the macro-dynamics of museum-making in other countries and contexts.

Museums and Nationalism in Croatia, Hungary, and Turkey provides rare and interesting insights into how museums materialise culture in the service of nationalism. The book will be of interest to those engaged in the study of museums, heritage, nationalism, memory, and politics, as a result.

Lorenzo Posocco holds a dual PhD in sociology from the University College Dublin (UCD) and political science from the École des Hautes Études en Sciences Sociales Paris (EHESS). He was a visiting researcher in Istanbul at Yeditepe University and Graz at the Centre for Southeast European Studies. Currently, he is a research assistant in UCD and collaborates with the University of Rome Tor Vergata where he teaches in the Department of History, Cultural Heritage, Education and Society.

Museums and Nationalism in Croatia, Hungary, and Turkey

Lorenzo Posocco

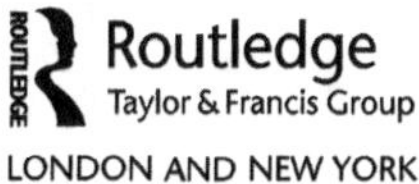

LONDON AND NEW YORK

First published 2022
by Routledge
2 Park Square, Milton Park, Abingdon, Oxon OX14 4RN

and by Routledge
605 Third Avenue, New York, NY 10158

Routledge is an imprint of the Taylor & Francis Group, an informa business

British Library Cataloguing-in-Publication Data
A catalogue record for this book is available from the British Library

Library of Congress Cataloging-in-Publication Data
A catalog record for this book has been requested

ISBN: 978-0-367-51247-7 (hbk)
ISBN: 978-0-367-51248-4 (pbk)
ISBN: 978-1-003-05303-3 (ebk)

DOI: 10.4324/9781003053033

Typeset in Times New Roman
by Apex CoVantage, LLC

I dedicate this book to the memory of those men, women, elderly, and children who have suffered unspeakable suffering, humiliation, and death in the name of nationalism and its racist aberration, only to be thrown into the mass grave of history. Forgotten. And to those who fight against that same ideology in the present, so that fragments of those stories re-emerge from oblivion and trace the path towards a more human humanity.

Contents

Figures

Acknowledgements

Many people played a role, in one way or another, in helping me to develop this study, and therefore deserve my deepest gratitude. The first is my mentor and friend Iarfhlaith Watson. I don’t exaggerate when I say that this book would not exist without his support and help. The same is true for Siniša Malešević, who guided me through the publication process from when the book was just an idea in an embryonic state. I am extremely grateful to both of them also for taking the time to read the manuscript and for their precious advice. I am grateful also to Elizabeth Crooke for inviting me to the 5th Biennial Conference of the Association of the Critical Heritage Studies (ACHS) last year. Presenting part of this work at the conference provided useful critiques that contributed to improve the manuscript. Special thanks go to Saša Božić, Andrea Pető, Erin Jenne, Ivan Roško, İnci Bilgiç, Muhammed Akif Serdar, Hazal Arda, and Eszter Molnár. Without their invaluable support, the fieldwork wouldn’t have been possible.

I would like to thank the editors at Routledge for helping me through the publication of this book. Finally, I would like to thank my family, in particular my wife, for her love and superhuman patience. I am aware it takes plenty of both to stand by me.

Introduction

Nationalism's way through the museum

On February 24, 2002, Hungary's Prime Minister Viktor Orbán stood in front of a crowd of 30,000 people outside the House of Terror Museum in Budapest. The event marked its inauguration. The museum found room in a building that symbolised both fascist and communist crimes in Hungary, where the Arrow Cross Party (1944–45) and ÁVH (appendage of the Soviet Union's secret police forces, 1945–1956) detained, interrogated, tortured, or killed their victims. Desired by Prime Minister Orbán, this museum soon fell under the spotlight as one of the ideological cabinets of his national-conservative party, Fidesz, for emphasising the crimes of communists, playing down the ones of fascists, and softening Hungary's role in the Holocaust (Radonić, 2020). The night Orbán inaugurated the museum, a stage had been set outside in front of the museum building. The footage[1] shows Orbán walking in and taking the stage, people clapping, and someone screaming out of excitement. The Hungarian Prime Minister looks down, trying to remain focused on his speech, and holds a microphone in his hands.

> in this building there is a great power, sacrifice, belonging, the power of our nation . . . although many feel that what happened here needs vengeance, after the collapse of socialism, those who suffered the terror had the power to say no to it. The sacrificed, humiliated, parents, brothers, children, those who survived gave us the possibility to restore the independence of our nation, the freedom of its citizens

Eighteen years later, on July 10, 2020, Turkey's President Recep Tayyip Erdoğan stood in front of a camera announcing the reconversion of the ancient basilica of Hagia Sophia from museum to mosque, undoing what the first president of Turkey, Mustafa Kemal Atatürk—icon of Turkish secularism—had done more than 80 years earlier. An extract of his speech reports: 'after a gap of 86 years Hagia Sophia will serve as a mosque again . . . it is the sovereign right of Turkey to decide the purpose of Hagia

DOI: 10.4324/9781003053033-1

Sophia'.[2] Around two weeks later, Erdoğan also attended the first prayer in the new-old mosque, together with 350,000 people in the surrounding area. Ali Erbas, head of the Presidency of Religious Affairs in Turkey, guided the *khutbah* (sermon): 'Today is the day when believers stand for prayers in tears, bow down in peace, and prostrate in gratitude. . . . Endless praise be to God Almighty . . . who enabled us to appear before him in this great Hagia Sophia. Peace and salutations be to Prophet Muhammad, who gave the good news about the conquest, saying "One day Constantinople will be conquered"'.[3]

What do these events, separated by years and occurring in two different social, cultural, and political contexts have in common? What is the relation between the museum and the nationalist rhetoric of Orbán and Erdoğan? Why did these politicians, who are widely recognised as marking a nationalist shift in their countries, choose museums as the stage for nationalist speeches? Are these isolated events, or is there a structural correlation between nationalism and museums? If yes, how can it be defined? To what extent do museums, as legitimate and legitimising recipients of historical memory, contribute to the reproduction of national narratives, and with them, the reproduction of the nation-state as the political expression of the nation?

This book attempts to answer these and other questions regarding the relationship between nationalism and museums. The underlying reason is that a rich body of literature on nationalism emerged in the recent years that might change our understanding of this relationship. The starting point is the acknowledgement that, although liberal capitalism, globalisation, and cosmopolitanism are changing the world, nation-states seem to be here to stay and nationalism—the ideology giving birth to an imaginary representation of the self as a national self immersed in a world appearing, naturally, as a world of nation—remains the 'dominant mode of political legitimacy and collective subjectivity in the modern era' (Malešević, 2019: 7). Moreover, nationalism studies have stressed an ideological, penetrating, and organisational capacity of nationalism that was unacknowledged until recently. This scholarship returns a scenario where nationalism is present at all levels of society, in state infrastructures, communication networks, bureaucracy as well as in the micro-interactional universe of people, thus in people's everyday lives as integral to the interaction practices of individuals through national languages and symbols that are recognisable and shared by all. Investigating the museum through this lens is to acknowledge that the influence of nationalism weighs heavier than previously thought, and goes well beyond the construction of national museums by political elites. These ideas, on which other recent studies on memory and remembrance such as Lea David's The Past Can't Heal Us (2020) are based, shape the lens through which I look at the phenomenon of nationalism in the museum. For the sake of clarity, this book was inspired by scholars—among others, Aronsson and Elgenius (2015), Smith (2006), Watson et al. (2019), Macdonald (2003), and Bennett (1995), just to mention a few—who paved the way integrating theories of nationalism in their studies on the museum. Their significant contributions in this area are the material proof of the great value of interdisciplinarity. I'll critically review this solid body of literature, including the theories on nationalism, museum, and nationalism in museums in a separate chapter (Chapter 1).

Drawing on this literature, the goal of the book is to question the deeply embedded idea that museums are 'democratising, inclusive and polyphonic spaces for critical dialogue . . . not for profit . . . participatory and transparent and work to . . . contribute to human dignity and social justice, global equality and planetary wellbeing' (International Council of Museums-ICOM, 2019). This definition, endorsed by the UNESCO, UN, and others, represents an ideal museum, not what the museum actually is. Although its goals are embraceable and worth struggling for, to think of the museum as an ideal place, detached from the heteronomous forces that gravitate around and enter it, poses some problems. The work of museum directors, curators, architects, external consultants, museum committees, and reviewers of the museum appointed and influenced by political forces with nationalist agendas might (and do) clash with ICOM's ideal museum. Moreover, in addition to the conscious attempts to permeate the museum with nationalist politics, one must consider the omnipresence of "banal nationalism" in everyday life (Billig, 1995; Skey, 2009; Fox, 2018; Fox and Miller-Idriss, 2008) that includes the use of flags in everyday contexts, national sporting events, national songs, national currency, national music, national academies, the use of implied togetherness and otherness in expressions such as "us" and "them". These elements give body to the nation and are most effective because of their subliminal nature, mostly unnoticed. This is one of the features of ideology, therefore of nationalism, as Žižek put it: it runs ubiquitously through society and everybody is influenced even when they think they aren't (Žižek, 1989). In this perspective, nationalism inevitably affects those professionals appointed to materially make the museum, its architecture and installations. Overlooking the structural and subjective forces of nationalism means turning a blind eye to the conflicts they generate, hampering the search for solutions, and carrying the risk that ICOM's ideal museum remains precisely what it is, only an ideal. With this in mind, if I was forced to define the biggest endeavour of this book, it would be the attempt to identify and interrogate these forces. They represent the key to investigate the macro and micro, structural and subjective dynamics that make all museums national museums, even when they aren't.

This work of identification and analysis took, for the case studies investigated in this book, almost 2 years of fieldwork in three countries, Turkey, Hungary, and Croatia, and around 50 in-depth interviews, although the number of people I met and talked to is higher. It required travelling before and after the coup d'etat that hit Turkey in 2016, asking permission for interviews with politicians and bureaucrats that often took months to be accepted, when they weren't rejected. This happened too. The nature of this research provoked, although rarely, harsh reactions on the part of interviewees who felt threatened by it. This occurred even when the study ensured them full anonymity and provided a statement of ethical approval signed by my academic institution. Once, I was told by a state official not to write about a specific museum and was explicitly threatened if I did. It also happened that I have been "accompanied" by a person specifically sent by the Ministry of Culture to make sure that my interviewees' statements reflected what the government expected from them, and when these expectations weren't met, I was told to modify my questions. These events reinforced my conviction that politics, and nationalism with it, is an inextricable part of the museum, even for those that do not fall within the category of "national museum". Nationalism, especially in its extreme forms, doesn't like to be questioned. Although museums are not exactly places known as the quintessence of violence, one would be surprised by the struggles that unfold in museums around matters that to many might have no importance whatsoever. Some even lost their jobs. The hundreds of academics who, in Turkey and Hungary, lost their positions or were jailed for not complying with their governments' authoritarian policies suggest that this assumption might have some validity. As an example, I could refer to one of my interviewees, a historian, who fought against the request of politicised staff of the museum that asked him to soften the role that the museum attributed to the country in the Holocaust. This book is also dedicated to those who, like him, felt their duty to honour the memory of innocents, including children and the elderly, who suffered unutterable pains, insults, and humiliations before being brutally murdered. He, and others like him, stood in between the memory of these victims and a new "banal evil", to use the expression by Hannah Arendt, which plans to erase it. That said, ICOM's attempt to build a democratising, inclusive, and polyphonic museum is an important and necessary endeavour. This book goes towards the same direction as an attempt to give voice to the often-unheard stories of those who struggle to give body to this museum. To these and other events, I dedicate the three central chapters, one for each country under investigation.

With regards to the choice of Turkey, Croatia, and Hungary, under Orbán's and Erdoğan's governments, both Hungary and Turkey went through deep changes that affected these countries' museums. As detailed in their dedicated chapters (Chapters 3 and 5), in Hungary and Turkey changing narratives in museums have much to do with new national ideologies that carry a new vision of the past, present, and future of the nation incarnated in and matching with the one of new political elites. The goal is to investigate if, how, and to what extent this is true. With regards to Croatia, my attention was drawn by the fact that Croatian museums remain rather silent about those events that irrevocably changed the country, such as WW2, the communist era, and the end of communism. In Hungary, these same events are the centre of real cultural wars fought at all levels of society. This posed the question of whether Croatia's immobility in terms of exhibits and museums that have to do with pivotal moments in national history has any specific reason. In addition, the fact that Orbán's and Erdoğan's governments, especially after 2016, turned increasingly authoritarian, while Plenković's government in Croatia contained the push of the extremist fringes within his coalition, made these countries interesting case studies for comparison. Museums, as I attempt to prove, are affected by similar dynamics in the political sphere. Finally, the book considers more than 15 museums in three countries, although "only" 10 have been the focus of deep investigations, which meant tracing back and interviewing those who built them and the people who work/worked in them. That said, the choice of the museums followed one logic, that they shouldn't be national museums in the traditional sense as museums purposely created to exhibit about the nation. The declared goal of the study is to look at the way nationalism worms its way into museums that aren't necessarily "national". This choice is reflected in the variety of museum categories under investigation: science museums, art museums (Kunsthalle), photography museums, war museums, Holocaust museums, and history museums.

In Hungary, these museums are the Holocaust Memorial and Documentation Center (HDKE), the House of the Hungarian Millennium, and the Kunsthalle. The HDKE is one of those positive examples of museum that successfully overcame external pressure from politicians with a nationalist agenda aimed to downplay Hungary's role in the Holocaust. As for all museums in this study, the investigation of this museum looks at the way nationalism worms or attempts to worm its way in. The HDKE was inspired by archetypical museums such as Yad Vashem and the US Holocaust Memorial Museum. In the 21st century, these became real points of reference, setting a standard in Holocaust memorialisation. As a museum that exhibits evidence of mass human rights abuse perpetrated by the Nazis and the Hungarian people, and as one that performs its function rather successfully, the HDKE became the target of Orban's nationalist regime. The latter attempted to make it conform to other museums that, like the House of Terror Museum, espouse, so to say, a less critical view on the nation. Besides the dynamics that brought this museum to resist the nationalist attack of the government, the comparison between the HDKE and another memorial museum, this time in Croatia, the Jasenovac Memorial Site Museum, will provide interesting data on the way different political settings respond to similar museums. In fact, unlike the HDKE that aroused the government's attention, the memorial in Jasenovac was accused by nongovernmental forces of being too lenient in the representations of the crimes committed by the Ustaše, the Croatian Revolutionary Movement, during WW2.

Another museum investigated in Chapter 3 is the House of the Hungarian Millennium, which is part of a larger project that is changing one of the most iconic parks of Budapest, Városliget City Park, and includes the ongoing building of four additional museums. The House of the Hungarian Millennium is a history museum resuming the celebration for the 1,000 year anniversary of the establishment of the Hungarian state in 1896. In this perspective, it is one of those museums that give body to national myths, attempting to provide historical substance to the idea that the birth of the Hungarian nation can be traced back centuries. This institution fits well within the national ideology of Orban's party, Fidesz, which sees in the 19th century, the era when the celebration for the millennium took place, the golden age of Hungary. Looking at this museum, the only one among the five built so far, I will attempt to understand what kind of mark Orban's nationalist agenda is leaving on the museum landscape in Hungary, and how.

In addition to the House of the Hungarian Millennium, I will look at an art museum, the Kunsthalle, which serves as an example of a different category of museum influenced by nationalism. One of the most progressive art galleries in Europe before the coming to power of Fidesz in 2010, the Kunsthalle turned increasingly conservative after a new museum director was appointed whose ideas were more in line with the government's ideal of art. In addition, governmental decisions seem to have affected the Hungarian art scene negatively, so much so as to prompt heated public debates and even gave birth to anti-governmental art Biennale, the OFF-Biennale, officially launched by artists and gallerists contrary to the overwhelming presence of the state into the affairs of Hungary's art community.

In the chapter dedicated to Croatia (Chapter 5), besides looking at the Jasenovac Memorial Site Museum, this book will focus on the Image of War Museum. This is a photography museum focusing on the 1991–1995 war between Croatian independentists and the Serb-led Yugoslav army. Its peculiarity is that it was designed with the goal of challenging the idea of nationalist representations of the war. Through interviews with curators, the museum director, and personnel of the museum, this study will attempt to investigate the process of challenging nationalism and understand whether it was successful or not. Finally, another case study will investigate the 1980s Museum, a privately owned museum designed in an apartment in Croatia's capital Zagreb, whose goal is reviving life under socialism. Besides reflecting the fact that, as Hooper-Greenhill (1992) wrote almost 30 years ago, nowadays almost anything can be turned into a museum, this case study attempts to show the promptness with which nationalist entrepreneurs take the chance of giving body to positive representations of nationalism. In this case, as I will detail in Chapter 5, the first version of this museum was bought by a Chinese delegation in a diplomatic mission in Croatia and it is now travelling through China to show Chinese people how good life was in communist Croatia. In addition, I will show how the museum was led by the principle of economic profit and how it functioned as a launch platform for profitable mutual relations between the Chinese and Croatian governments.

In Turkey, I looked at the Panorama Museum 1453, Kabatepe Simulation Center and Museum, Istanbul Museum of Science and Technology in Islam, and Istanbul Military Museum. All of them look predominantly at Turkey's Ottoman heritage, which has been, and still is, a strategic element of Erdoğan's cultural policy. This heritage, as Jenny White (2009) already noticed, plays an important role in reshaping the national identity of modern Turks, which reflects the one of a pious Muslim Turk whose past dives in the splendours of the empire revived in a republican setting. This is understood as a divorce from Kemalism, carried out silently (Tuğal, 2009), without massive shock, at least before the coup d'état that almost dethroned Erdoğan and whose failure ended up raising him even higher, symbolically at least, almost to the rank of Sultan (Cagaptay, 2017). Museums as I see them served Erdoğan as the historical legitimation of his nationalist vision. For this reason, his administration was always keen on supporting the building of new museums or the "restructuring" of others. The fact that three among four museums under investigation in this book reflect the prominence of war narratives in Turkey, hence narratives that espouse a romantic ethnic version of nationalism as the myth of blood, descent, martyrdom, and conquest, is no coincidence. Turks as the heirs of warriors that won their land, and therefore must preserve it, is one of the pillars of Erdoğanism. Two of the battles that all Turks know about are the conquest of Constantinople in 1453 (Panorama Museum 1453), which is the founding myth of the Ottoman Empire, and the battle of the Dardanelles (Kabatepe Simulation Center and Museum), which marks the end of this empire and heralds the beginning of the Turkish Republic. What this study attempts to do is investigate how Erdoğan's administration inserts itself into these narratives, building around them new museums that reflect the national ideology of the party, reshaping them in a way most convenient to their political agenda. With regard to the Istanbul Museum of the History of Science and Technology in Islam, it is a case study that shows how the Justice and Development Party, Erdoğan's party, struggles to convince Turks (and everybody else) that Islam and modernity did, and can still, go hand in hand, that Islam is not the equivalent of backward, and that indeed, as the heritage of Turkey, Islam is something Turks should be proud of. Finally, the Istanbul Military Museum differentiates itself (at least on paper) from the previous case studies insofar as it is a museum managed by the Turkish army. Historically, the Turkish army was always loyal to the Kemalist secular tradition, thus ideologically distant from Erdoğanism, although they also converge when coming to aspects such as a certain tendency to authoritarianism. However, comparing narratives such as the conquest of Constantinople and the battle of the Dardanelles, both present in the Istanbul Military Museum, I will attempt to show that in spite of ideological differences, they don't change much, if at all. Certain narratives are part of the national baggage of stories and myths that are deeply entrenched in national tradition and remain almost untouched, serving multiple nationalist ideologies. In addition, by analysing the temporary exhibition on the forty-first anniversary of the war in Cyprus, this case study will attempt to shed light on the techniques of historical negationism or denialism that are also used in the context of the museum.

Finally, although this book focuses on nationalism, other heteronomous forces within and across the museum can and often do affect it. With "heteronomous forces" I mean all those forces that are supposed to be external to the museum and yet undermine ICOM's ideal that the museum should be non-profit, independent, and so on. Capitalism and financial profit is one of them, but also globalisation, with its flows of people and goods, and cosmopolitanism with its load of internationalism play a role. Especially in Chapters 3 and 4 I look superficially at nationalism and capitalism as two forces that sometimes intertwine. However, deeper investigations would require a separate publication. There simply isn't enough space in this book. In addition, I gave priority to collecting as much evidence as possible about the variegated presence and the tenacity of nationalism in the museum. I hope that in the future there will be room for research that attempts a more systematic study of how all these forces act and interact within the museum.

Notes

1 The footage is publicly available on YouTube at the following address: www.youtube.com/watch?v=DAQpHYU3m3s (Last Accessed 07/06/2021)

2 Full speech and footage at www.youtube.com/watch?v=bBvfWJecsxc (Last accessed 05/03/2021)

3 Full footage at www.youtube.com/watch?v=_UxPlw3PhzQ (Last accessed 20/05/2021)

1 Nationalism and the museum

Chapter 1 outlines the body of theories that guides this research on the relationships between nationalism and the museum in Turkey, Croatia, and Hungary. Its goal is to critically review scholarly studies that deal with this subject. The discussion starts with questioning the definition of museum given by the International Council of Museums (ICOM) and stresses the difference between the ideal museum of ICOM, a non-profit institution at the service of society, and the real one, an institution subject to heteronomous forces that influence it. The chapter continues with the identification of nationalism as ideology and one of the major forces impacting the museum. After providing the definitions of nationalism and nation-state, the chapter will look at the available literature on nationalism, museum, and nationalism in museum to acknowledge that nationalism is ubiquitous, present at all levels of society, structural and subjective, also in the museum, regardless of its typology, and the museum personnel.

What is a museum and what are the relationships between museums and nationalism? Being that the museum institution is more than 200 years old, one may think that there is a fairly clear idea of how to answer these questions. However, both the literature and the available definitions of museum show no consensus (Mason et al., 2018). A recent definition by the International Council of Museums (ICOM, 2019) highlights the purest purposes of the museum:

> Museums are democratising, inclusive and polyphonic spaces for critical dialogue about the pasts and the futures. Acknowledging and addressing the conflicts and challenges of the present, they hold artefacts and specimens in trust for society, safeguard diverse memories for future generations and guarantee equal rights and equal access to heritage for all people. Museums are not for profit. They are participatory and transparent, and work in active partnership with and for diverse communities to collect, preserve, research, interpret, exhibit, and enhance

DOI: 10.4324/9781003053033-2

> understandings of the world, aiming to contribute to human dignity and social justice, global equality and planetary wellbeing.
>
> (ICOM, International Council of Museums, 2019)

A second definition instead, officially acknowledges the political role of the museum, which is described as a dynamic institution—one that changes—according to the changing needs of society.

> Museums are dynamic and accountable public institutions which both shape and manifest the consciousness, identities and understandings of communities and individuals in relation to their natural, historical and cultural environments, through collection, documentation, conservation, research and communication programmes that are responsive to the needs of society.
>
> (SAMA, South African Museums Association, 1999)

It is revealing and worth highlighting that SAMA's definition was written in 1999, when the country was passing from a past of segregationist policies against non-white citizens to the end of the Apartheid. SAMA felt the need to address the problems created by white nationalism—which espouses the belief that white people should develop and maintain a white racial and nationalist South Africa—in South African museums. These involved, among others, under-representing, misrepresenting or not representing at all the native population in South African museums.

Investigating the relationships between museum and nationalism involves questioning, as SAMA did, the role of nationalism. The first important distinction is between far-right nationalism and nationalism. Although the vast literature on far-right nationalism shows no consensus on how to define it or even exactly what to call it, I call here far-right nationalism the ideology commonly associated with racial supremacist, xenophobic, homophobic or transphobic organisations that share certain traits such as the tendency to authoritarianism and recurrence to violence also in extreme forms such as ethnic cleansing or genocide. Instead, nationalism can be defined as an ideology entailing the belief that the world is naturally divided into nations that have distinctive cultural and physical characteristics inscribing them on the human landscape over time. It doesn't necessarily involve violence, xenophobia, homophobia, and so on. As Malešević put it, 'notwithstanding the centuries of coercive bureaucratic pressure and mass ideologisation, individual human beings remain largely unenthusiastic about killing or dying for abstract nationalist principles' (Malešević, 2013b: 33).

For Althuser, all ideologies, therefore also nationalism, have no relation to what he defines as "real world" but provide a set of imaginary relationships of individuals to the real world that are necessary to interact with it (Althusser, 2001). We are always within ideology, and different ideologies are but different representations of our social and imaginary reality, 'not a representation of the Real itself' (Althusser, 2001: 109). Nationalism as the 'dominant mode of political legitimacy and collective subjectivity in the modern era' (Malešević, 2019: 17) creates an imaginary representation of the self as a national self immersed in a world appearing, naturally, as a world of nations. For the sake of clarity, the fact that nationalism does not represent the Althuserrian real itself doesn't mean that its consequences are not real. The consequences of Nazism as an aberration of nationalism were (and are) real to millions of victims of WW2, Holocaust, and genocides. Without resorting to examples of violence, one could say, as Calhoun did, that nationalism is real in its modelling of our everyday life, our habits, and with them the way we interact with the world (Calhoun, 1997).

The view that nationalism is dominant is in line with Žižek's idea that ideology runs ubiquitously through society and everybody is influenced even when they think they aren't (Žižek, 1989). Malešević (2010, 2012a, 2012b, 2013a, 2017, 2019) went further with a theoretical model that sheds light on the development of nationalism as an ideology grounded at all levels of society. Through an approach based on the Braudelian longue durée, Malešević details the way nationalism worms its way through the intellectuals and the economic and cultural elites, and it gradually incorporates other social groups, the middle classes, the bureaucratic organs of the state, army, police, workers, and so on. Nationalism becomes structure institutionalised in the state and develops an extensive organisational capacity. It offers a perspective of liberation and collective emancipation that not many ideologies have, and this is an element that increases its ideological penetration. Finally, it gives birth to a national imaginary and rhetoric 'of micro-level solidarity to continuously legitimise and mobilise social action of individuals under their control' (Malešević, 2019: 38). These three points: 1) organisational capacity, 2) ideological penetration, and 3) envelopment of micro-solidarity are the basis of nationalism as a grounded ideology.

On logical grounds museums, as any other public or private institution, do not escape nationalism. Museum personnel, curators, historians, architects, art historians, archaeologists, and all those figures that revolve around the museum world are affected by it. For the sake of clarity, there is a solid body of literature that inspired this study and brings further evidence about nationalism as ubiquitous and nationalism as influencing museum display, architecture, and symbolism. These studies are the grounds to go one step further and advance the hypothesis at the basis of this book, that all museums are national museums, even when they aren't.

The first body of studies includes Anderson (1991), who saw nationalism in 'language and discursive practices of print technology and print capitalism, allied to changes in our conceptions of time' (Smith, 2009: 14); Gellner (1983) saw it in the modern political and economic structures that have given birth to nations; Hall and Malešević (2013) have focused on the connections between war and nationalism; Hobsbawm and Ranger (1983) saw nationalism in invented traditions, museums, monuments, and nationalist intellectuals; Breuilly (1982), Mann (1995), Brubaker (1992), and Tilly (1996) saw it in modernity, in particular in its technological, bureaucratic, political, and economic changes. Michael Billig (1995) saw it in the daily—almost unnoticed—reproduction of identity discourses. Evolutionary psychologists saw it in the DNA, thus in genes that incline people to prefer others who are genetically similar to themselves (Rushton, 2005). Craig Calhoun identified nationalism in discursive formation, ergo in language that shapes consciousness (Calhoun, 1997). Media scholars have seen it in the internet, shaping communities in cyberspace (Eriksen, 2007). Ethnomethodologists have seen modern nations and nationalism as inextricably linked to cultural resources rooted in ancient ethnies. They challenged modernists, emphasising the fact that modern nations are the result of nationalists who select a past of popular resonance and patterning of pre-existing ethnohistories (Smith, 2009; Von Scheve and Salmela, 2014). Finally, Michael Billig and his wide legacy (Billig, 1995; Skey, 2009; Fox and Miller-Idriss, 2008) identified popular aspects of nationalism such as the use of flags in everyday life, national expressions at national football games, anthems, and so on.

The second body of studies includes those works on identity negotiation and construction in heritage and museums as institutions created to celebrate the nation (Watson et al., 2019; Macdonald, 2011; McLean, 2005, 2006; Newmann and McLean, 2006; Macdonald, 2003; Fyfe, 2011; Boswell and Evans, 1999). Although, to my knowledge, there isn't a study that provides a comprehensive theoretical framework that could successfully explain the multifaceted influence of nationalism over museums. Many fail to acknowledge that the ubiquity of nationalism is such that its influence on museums goes well beyond the political elites, forgetting that not always do those who materially make museum exhibits belong to the latter. Moreover, ubiquity and ideological penetration of nationalism are also at the center of a process that is far from being understood, that is the ease with which visitors accept national discourses. Failing to recognise that museums are not only a matter of elites pushed Gordon Fyfe (2011) to call "dominant ideology approach" the one that sees museums as the product of and performing a top-down imposition. The advocates of the dominant ideology approach take museums as rituals of state power aimed to reinforce and reproduce the state structure, including class inequalities, individual and collective identities, and so on (Duncan and Wallach, 1980; Meltzer, 1981; Bourdieu, 1984). This notwithstanding, the current literature on museums and nation-making abounds with many studies on museums as rituals to celebrate the nation.

Scorrano (2011) studied national representation at the museum of Sydney, Australia, Żychlińska and Fontana (2016) focused on the celebration of the Polish national identity at the Warsaw Rising Museum, Crow (2009) studied the way the Chilean *Museo Histórico Nacional* celebrated Chilean identity by narrating Chilean national history, and Sang-hoon (2020) investigated nationhood in the National Museum of Korea. Similar case studies have been carried out almost everywhere by scholars of the museum. Finally, it was Crooke who, in *Museums and Community: Ideas, Issues and Challenges*, identified the importance of using the study of nationalism as a means to understanding museums. She wrote:

> Using the study of nationalism as a means to understanding museums reveals important aspects of their significance. The values that made museums useful for nationalism are the same characteristics that give them relevance today. Although the collections that we form today may be very different from those created by our predecessors in the eighteenth and nineteenth centuries, the reasons why we collect are much the same. Today, as in the past, collections are an expression of our identity. As we build collections they become an extension of ourselves; they reflect what we are interested in, our values, and our judgements.
>
> (Crooke, 2007: 14)

Similarly, for Elgenius, 'as part of the nexus of symbolism, used by elites as political tools, national museums raise awareness of, claim and contribute to the construction of national identities' (Elgenius, 2015: 145). Elgenius emphasises the role of the elites while Crooke uses the word "we" to include all those who contribute to the making of museums. It's an important distinction in the conceptualisation of the museum, but the basic point stands. Both definitions highlight the fact that museums reflect the society around them. Crooke states that museums reflect what we are interested in, our values, and our judgements. It appears that beliefs, values, and judgements are the building blocks of ideology. It follows that nationalism as the dominant ideology of our time is reflected in the museums we build.

Another study that proves useful when looking at the connections between nation and museums is Laurajane Smith's Use of Heritage (Smith, 2006). Building on other seminal works—among which are Bennett's *Birth of the Museum* (1995), Hooper-Greenhill's *Museums and the Shaping of Knowledge* (1992), and Duncan's *Civilizing Rituals* (1995)—Smith states:

> There is a hegemonic 'authorized heritage discourse', which is reliant on the power/knowledge claims of technical and aesthetic experts, and institutionalised in state cultural agencies and amenity societies. This discourse takes its cue from the grand narratives of nation and class on the one hand, and technical expertise and aesthetic judgement on the other. The 'authorized heritage discourse' privileges monumentality and grand scale, innate artefact/site significance tied to time depth, scientific/aesthetic expert judgement, social consensus, and nation-building.
> (Smith, 2006: 11)

The concept of "heritage" represents here all that's good and important about the past of the nation. It is what Smith defines as "authorized heritage", which is a discourse reliant on the kind of power/knowledge that museums claim to possess. Heritage is authorised when its subject and content are decided by "experts"—in Smith's words they are historians, archaeologists, architects, and museum curators—in the field of heritage. The concept of expert is defined here through the work of Michel Foucault (1966, 1975, 1991), whose studies have tackled problems arising from the relationship between knowledge, authority, and power. In Smith (and Foucault), power matches with elite and comes into play when, since the 19th century, states meteorically increased the use of disciplinary institutions such as the prison and psychiatric institutions, but also schools and museums. Smith, but also Macdonald (2003), Bennett (1995), and others show their awareness of museums as disciplinary institutions of the nation, where people learn about themselves as communities: nations in a world of nations. What they don't underline is that at the center of this discourse is always nationalism and that experts graduated from national schools and universities are the vehicles through which nationalism reproduces itself in museums and other public and private institutions. Charles Tilly made clear that in the world of nation-states education and nationalism are inextricable. National schools and academies impose standard national languages and produce national experts 'to organize expositions, museums, artistic subventions, and other means of displaying cultural production or heritage, to construct communication networks, to invent national flags, symbols, anthems, holidays, rituals, and traditions' (Tilly, 1994: 140). Similarly, Ulrich Beck and Andreas Wimmer wrote about methodological nationalism, which is the 'naturalization of the nation-state by the social sciences. Scholars who share this intellectual orientation assume that countries are the natural units for comparative studies, equate societies with the nation-state, and conflate national interests with the purposes of social sciences' (Wimmer and Glick Schiller, 2003: 576). Museums hire experts born into nations, educated in national schools and academies through national lenses, and subject to methodological nationalism. At this point, we must ask the following question: Is it surprising if the work of these experts reflects the national environment in which they were raised?

This brings us to the influence of nationalism over museums, which can be evident or subtle. In some typologies of museum, specifically in national museums, the mission is evident and public: to exhibit the national heritage. This typology of museum can be found in almost any state in the world. The Croatian History Museum in Zagreb, investigated in this book, is an example of a national museum. It will suffice to say that this typology of museum is inextricably linked to the birth of the modern nation-state; therefore, to states that endeavour to unite the people subjected to their rule 'by means of homogenisation, creating a common culture, symbols, values, reviving traditions and myths of origin, and sometimes inventing them' (Guibernau, 2003: 4). Here it is worth opening a brief parenthesis on the nation-state. It is a concept that will recur often in this book, and it is worth defining it to avoid misunderstanding. Nation-state is understood as the materialisation of the Gellnerian principle 'that the political and the national unit should be congruent' (Gellner, 1983: 1), thus ideally it is a territorial space occupied by one nation. For Brubaker, this territorial space is 'the dominant political reality of our time' (Brubaker, 2015: 115). It involves governments (democratic or not) that rule claiming to represent the nation, and nations believing to find expression in their states.[1] As a means of example, I report three extracts of this rhetoric from the constitutions of the case studies under scrutiny in this book:

> Affirming the eternal existence of the Turkish Motherland and Nation and the indivisible unity of the Sublime Turkish State, this constitution, in line with the concept of nationalism introduced by the founder of the Republic of Turkey, Ataturk, the immortal leader and the unrivalled hero, and his reforms and principles.
>
> (Turkish Constitution, 2017)

> The millennial national identity of the Croatian nation and the continuity of statehood, confirmed the course of its entire historical experience in various political forms and by the perpetuation and development of the state-building idea grounded in the historical right of the Croatian nation to full sovereignty, has manifested itself in . . .
>
> (Constitution of the Republic of Croatia, 2010)

> WE, THE MEMBERS OF THE HUNGARIAN NATION, at the beginning of the new millennium, with a sense of responsibility for every Hungarian, hereby proclaim the following . . . We are proud of the outstanding intellectual achievements of the Hungarian people . . . We commit to promoting and safeguarding our heritage, our unique language, Hungarian culture, the languages and cultures of nationalities living in Hungary . . .
>
> (The Fundamental Law of Hungary, 2011)

This kind of nation-state rhetoric contributes to project the nation back into the past, creating a sense of common ethnic descent and brotherhood. Moreover, it legitimises the production of a similar national rhetoric not only in political settings, where it justifies the right of politicians to rule (Malešević, 2019), but also in cultural ones, especially in national museums. This is how the special category of national museums gets to absolve the function as producer and reproducer of national history to match the dominant nationalist rhetoric and goes so far as inventing a fictional past (Hobsbawm and Ranger, 1983). In this perspective, national museums are unique institutions placed as witnesses and performers of nation-building (Elgenius, 2015). They 'illuminate, through collections and displays, that which Anderson (1991) identified as "imagined" or Hobsbawm called an "invented tradition"' (Elgenius, 2015: 145).

Besides the specific category of national museums there are many other museums dedicated to various subjects: archaeology, art, science, music, war, and so on. In Zagreb there is a museum of mushrooms and one of broken relationships that demonstrate how Hooper-Greenhill (1992) was right almost 30 years ago, when she said that nowadays almost anything can be turned in a museum. Outlining all of them doesn't fall within the scope of this study. What is worth underlying is that, although they aren't officially national museums, their display and architecture involves a large variety of national symbols, references in information panels, object descriptions, and even their position within the museum often follows national logics. As born in a world of nation-states, most of the objects within them are framed within national lenses (Italian painters, Turkish poets, Hungarian music, food, etc.), so much so that science becomes national science, art becomes national art, religion becomes national religion, food, and so on. In doing so, these museums contribute to reproduce the nation even if they haven't been specifically created for that. Theories of nationalism such as Michael Billig's Banal Nationalism (1995) support and make sense of this phenomenon, suggesting that it is the daily bombardment of national references in all spheres and fields of society that ensures that people take nationalism for granted. Paradoxically one could argue that because nationalism is everywhere it achieves a certain degree of invisibility. For Shelton (2013), whose praxiological museology inspired this book, the goal of a critical museology is to reveal exactly this kind of invisibility within museums, not only what is manifest. Critical museology is 'to sustain an ongoing critical and dialectical dialogue that endangers a constant self-reflective attitude toward museum practices and their wider constituencies' (Shelton, 2013: 18). The necessity of such a dialogue, which involves a critical eye on museum practice, lies in what I just highlighted, thus the alarming capacity of nationalism entering the museum without leaving much trace, becoming 'invisible through repetition and seeming "normal"' (Mason et al., 2018: 22). In the perspective of this study on nationalism and museums, espousing Shelton's approach means looking at the less evident and more subtle—although not less pervasive—ways in which nationalism worms its way into the museum.

One of these ways was suggested by Tony Bennett, who investigated what he called the self-monitoring system of looks where 'the subject and object positions can be exchanged, in which the crowd comes to commune with and regulate itself through interiorizing the ideal and ordered view of itself as seen from the controlling vision of power' (Bennett, 1995: 69). This is, in a nutshell, Bennett's concept of "exhibitionary complex", for which people are placed on the side of power, turning the museum into the people's subject and beneficiary (Bennett, 1995, 2004, 2015b). If one replaces the word "people" with "nation" the utility of this concept for a study on nationalism and museum emerges. Through the exhibitionary complex the nation becomes the subject and recipient of the museum. Nationals are invited to think of the museum as their museum and the collections within it as national collections, even when they aren't. Historically, this wasn't always the case. Before the nation-state, royal collections belonged to royal families and were meant to glorify the royal elites vis-à-vis a public that most of the time was composed of elites (Hooper-Greenhill, 1992; Bennett, 1995). Nationalism has reversed all this. In the era of nation-states all museums are meant to glorify the nation, much less criticise it. This is also true in museums whose reputation is linked to their international collections (such as the Louvre, British Museum, Pergamon Museum, Hermitage, etc.) or those that promote "world cultures" rather than "national ones", as Watson and Sawyer claimed for museums in Britain (Watson and Sawyer, 2011). They all remain national realities inscribed within the nation-state, and as such are often advertised nurturing national pride [Figure 1.1].

National self-glorification occurs in a setting that shares many elements with ceremonial monuments of the kind of churches, shrines, and temples. This similarity between sacred institutions and museums was already noticed by Duncan and Wallach (1980) and Bourdieu (1993), both in reference to the art museum. The concept of the museum as an institution

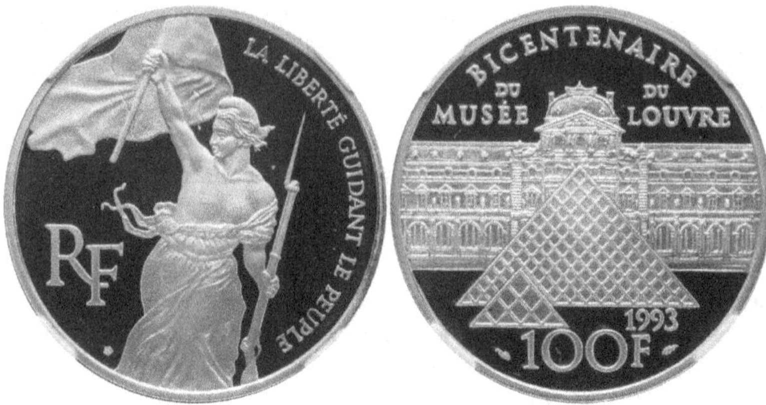

Figure 1.1 Two sides of a toke. On one side, the "Marianne", symbol of the French nation. On the other, the Louvre. This is one of many examples of museums that, although they exhibit international collections, become national symbols.

consecrating the nation is in line with Gellner's idea that 'In a nationalist age, societies worship themselves brazenly and openly, spurning the camouflage' (Gellner, 1983: 56). On a similar line, Frank Wright wrote that nationalisms are religions (Wright, 1988: 75). If this is true, then we can think of museums as ceremonies of nationalism mediating between the deity, which is the nation, and citizens, who by worshipping it worship themselves. The museum would be both a symbol and a ritual of the nation, as Duncan suggests in her study of the Louvre (Duncan, 2013). Another scholar who contributed to our understanding of museums as 'providing the scenography and stage for the performance of myths of nationhood' is Simon Knell (2011: 6). This literature helps us to make sense of a museum where the nation participates, as a protagonist, in the national ritual. National stories are told, national emotions are felt, and the virtues of nations are celebrated together with modern national heroes, be they painters, sculptors, soldiers, politicians, poets, or writers. Museums chant their deeds, deepen their life stories, magnify their work, and sometimes reproduce it on a larger scale, as past societies did with colossal statues of gods. In an almost sacred setting, where a religious silence is forced upon the visitor and the prohibition to touch the objects is enforced, visitors find their place, beside their national heroes, in a world of nations. This world makes sense to them; it is as evident as the gods to the ancient Greeks and Romans. In this way, the museum becomes a stage where the national world is self-evident. It is a world that goes without saying. This theatrical stage where the nation is often an unnoticed but ever present protagonist turns all museums into an expression of nationalism. With this in mind, the museum can be seen as a construct of both the first and second order. The existence of the museum as the symbolism within it echoes nationalism, their buildings and symbols echo nationalism, and they produce and reproduce it on a daily basis. This is one of the most interesting aspects of the museum as an institution of the nation-state. It is perfectly integrated into its ideological discourses and organisational structures, contributing to always new cycles of nation-building.

Note

1 This is a delusion. The state doesn't represent the nation but a limited number of social agents that sit in power positions in public affairs (Bourdieu, 2014).

2 Methodology and sample

A qualitative research methodology has been used for this study. Qualitative studies distinguish themselves by capturing and presenting what is or was going on in one or a few "cases" of socially significant phenomena in depth. They are rich in descriptions or narratives of cultural, emotional, and social life, sometimes in a comparative framework (Goodwin and Horowitz, 2002: 35). Among many specialised uses of qualitative research, this study employed one-to-one in-depth interviews with individuals from specialised groups, direct observation, analysis of transcripts, and other texts as well as various audio and visual elements. As I aimed to collect data about the construction of new national narratives in national museums, about the diverse specialised groups which play a role in this construction, and the way this construction contributes to produce and reproduce the nation, a qualitative methodology that combines in-depth interviews and the visual analysis of the museum seemed to me the best method to address my theoretical argument.

In combining different data sources, I learnt about both the backgrounds and roles of the social agents at play in the museum and the objective structures that, by encompassing them, constrain (but do not determine) their agency. Furthermore, the narrative of the museum included visual elements such as paintings, video, audio, and text, especially on information panels and brochures of the museum. Most of the chosen museums are relatively recent museums whose openings were accompanied by speeches of the President of the Republic, the Prime Minister, and other public figures whose discourses are freely available on the web. Those speeches represented a data source of discourses that I analysed. The combination of multiple data sources granted a multi-perspective view which displayed diverse sides of the museum. In particular, it helped to see it from the point of view of those who commissioned it and those who made it. In this view, I could investigate whether elites with a nationalist agenda were behind the commissioning of the museum, whether and how the museum functioned as a

DOI: 10.4324/9781003053033-3

place of production of national narratives, and to what extent nationalism was embraced and therefore reproduced or contested by those who made the museum.

Method of interview

Respondents were interviewed by using a semi-structured method which entailed the development of a list of questions and topics that were covered during our conversation. Unlike structured interviews, semi-structured interviews involve open questions that allow the respondent some autonomy in further developing the points raised by the researcher. This way, the interviewer can ask additional questions in response to the interviewee's answers. This allowed me to shift, when needed, from the previously arranged questions and follow paths that were not previously considered. In this view, semi-structured interviews are used when the researcher has designed a research hypothesis which seeks validation but is still open to unexpected findings. This method happened to be particularly useful in interviewing specialised groups such as the ones I targeted: historians and politicians. In interviewing specialists, each interview guided the future of the interview process itself; it provided both the contacts for future interviews and crucial information which would otherwise be unavailable. In this study on the museum, this included the name of the artistic producers, historians, archaeologists, and architects who took part in its building as internal or external consultants, the financial nature of the museum, the staff, museum directors, curators, their roles and hierarchies, the relations between them, sensitive data concerning the private and working life of public people, and so on. It was impossible to have this information beforehand; therefore, it was very unlikely that I could define the interviewee sample before the fieldwork. We are faced, as Baab states, with a process of discovery (Baab et al., 2012), thus I needed as much flexibility as possible, and semi-structured interviews provided that.

Sample of participants and data collection

A central difference between sample survey interviewing and interviewing individuals from the elite and from specialised groups is the degree to which the interview and the sample of participants is standardised (Baab et al., 2012: 302). That does not mean we cannot identify potential interviews or design interviews beforehand; in fact, I did sample my interviewees on the basis of the chosen museums. My interviews targeted curators, archaeologists, historians, and museum directors of the chosen museums, while I used secondary data sources for politicians' discourses and interviews.

After having collected information that is usually publicly available about those who commissioned the museum, I attempted to organise interviews with them. In these interviews, one of the questions I always asked was on the number of people who took part in the making of the museum, who they were, and if the interviewee could introduce me to them. Precisely because this method involves a process of discovery, the sample of interviewees was adjusted during the research process.

Qualitative research can pose different problems, especially when carried out in a foreign country. I was unsure about the permission from the museum to carry out interviews with the staff and I was unsure whether I would have been granted permission for filming the museum interior. Another problem concerned the political administration whose busy agenda or unwillingness to talk could undermine the feasibility of the research. For example, the political and social crisis of Turkey worsened the situation in which this study was carried out. Just a few weeks before my first fieldwork in Southern Turkey (in the city of Diyarbakir), a civil war erupted between the Kurdish minority and the Turkish state. As tension rose, a museum I had aimed to examine was closed and the artefacts were put in a safe place. I had become an acquaintance of the person who owned the company that had built the museum. She advised me not to go because, in her words, "people are being shot on the street". The authoritarianism of the government grew, and also hit academia, which raised its voice in 2015, supported by names like Noam Chomsky, Immanuel Wallerstein, and David Harvey. This happened when the judiciary prosecuted 37 academics for having signed a petition against the military operations in the southeast (Human Rights Watch, 2016). Fortunately, this first phase of fieldwork finished one week before the attempted coup d'état of July 15, 2016, when I flew back home. However, the tension in the Turkish administration due to the clenching hold of the AKP was evident even before the coup and made public officers more cautious. Any research that took a critical look at the state was looked upon with suspicion and most of the museum directors asked me to seek the permission of the Ministry of Culture. The Ministry would ask about the reasons for the research, and in some cases, would appoint some ministry officers to physically control the interview process.

Even when the interview was accepted, a variety of other issues arose. First of all, trust. Especially in interviews with state administrators, 'interviewers need to gain the trust of their respondents in order to collect high quality data' (Harvey, 2009: 433). The language and even my identity as a foreigner could represent an insurmountable barrier to gain trust from the respondent. The situation improved when I was granted an affiliation with a Turkish university, Yeditepe University, which included funding from Tübitak—The Turkish Research Council. This allowed me to present the study as state-sponsored research, creating trust with respondents who then showed themselves more willing to collaborate and stopped asking if I had permission from the ministry. Leaflets and informed consents explained the research in detail and were emailed to the museum. The Tübitak logo was visible on the front page and a Turkish gatekeeper contacted the museums in my name. However, this did not always result in the desired reaction. For the interviewee, to sign meant to leave a trace; therefore, many refused and suggested a more relaxed and overall "unofficial" talk without it being recorded.

I planned interviews following Baab's suggestion that 'researchers may find that the best initial interviews may be with people who are somewhat marginal to the situation, but who are viewed as neutral or "mainstream" by most participants' (Baab et al., 2012: 304). The Turkish fieldwork can function as an example here. My first interview was with the director of the research centre affiliated with the Istanbul Museum of the History of Science and Technology in Islam. He hadn't been that involved with the making of the museum, but had information to share. The interview was recorded, lasted about 1 hour and 20 minutes, and provided the study with data about the staff of the museum, its process of ideation and construction, the role of the administrations, the name of the historians, archaeologists, art historians, and artists involved in it, and information about the funding of the museum. Furthermore, as the respondent was an acquaintance of the museum director, I had permission to contact her in his name. I learned that this was the only modus operandi which produced good results. To be presented by an acquaintance helped decrease suspicion, which was at the highest level due to the political situation.

After interviewing the museum director, I could already compare the information given by the latter and the director of the research centre of the museum and consider their statements not only in terms of validity but also on the basis of their background, different roles, responsibility, and hierarchy within the museum. I followed a similar method at other museums in Turkey, Hungary, and Croatia. The goal was always to find a key person who could introduce us (me and my gatekeepers) to those they believed had the most information and the power to provide me with further contacts. Finally, we were granted access to all the museums under investigation, carried out interviews and filmed or photographed the museum interior, although not always without problems.

The most significant data came from interviews with curators and academics who worked at the museums as external consultants. Museum directors and bureaucrats in general would not expose themselves to critics and remained off the record most of the time. Instead, curators and academics seemed to value the study as an important contribution to the field of the museum. Usually, they provided me with more contacts and showed their availability for a second interview.

It often happened that interviewees who held a high position in the museum or in the political sphere didn't accept the interview or simply wouldn't bother answering calls or emails. Similar rejections also occurred in other museums and contexts. For the sake of clarity, most of the time, when I was not interviewing state servants who worked in/for museums, I was trying to reach them. It was a mistake, undervaluing the intricacies of bureaucracy. Had I known, for example, about the time spent on the phone with bureaucrats' secretaries, the paperwork required by the bureaucracy to interview museum directors and managers, the time spent waiting for their approval, the frustration vis-à-vis any refusal, I probably would have changed my research subject. Although at some point I learnt when and if to push for an official interview, and whether to ask to record or not. In hindsight, when thinking about the many problems that bureaucracy created, I ask myself, should I have known? The answer is no. The museum orthodoxy dictates that museums are places of culture, not bureaucracies. This particular subject, bureaucracy and museums, would be worthy of more space than is available in this book. I resolve to go into this topic in more depth in another context.

3 Nationalism and museums in Hungary

This chapter looks at the relationships between nationalism and museums in Hungary. It's divided into two sections. The first is a historical introduction from the 19th century to the present, whose primary goal is to provide the reader with a historical background on the Hungarian museum. This includes events around the process of nation-making in Hungary, WW1 and WW2, the communist and post-communist era, with particular attention to the recent years under Viktor Orbán's governments. The second section focuses on the in-depth investigation of the following museums: the Holocaust Memorial and Documentation Center (HDKE), a museum of the Holocaust located in Budapest; The House of the Hungarian Millennium, a recently built history museum in Budapest; and the Kunsthalle, an art museum. It brings evidence of the ruling government trying to influence the exhibit of the museum. The overall goal is to bring evidence about the way nationalism enters the museum and influences it.

The history of the museum institution in Hungary responds to what Tony Bennett called the 'constellations of national, sub-national, becoming national, supra-national dynamics imperial/colonial formations' (Bennett, 2015a: 68) that have marked the country in the last 200 years. The first Hungarian museum was the National Museum, constructed before the Hungarian nation-state, in 1803. Back then, Hungary was a kingdom subject to the rule of the larger Austrian Empire. The Emperor of Austria was also the King of Hungary, and the Hungarian foreign policy and army were one with the Austrian (Thorpe, 2015: 42). Additionally, the Hungarian elites—promoters of the museum institution—were integrated within the Austrian aristocracy. Most of them were educated in Vienna and often occupied positions within the imperial administration and the army (Apor, 2011: 405). These elites, who donated artefacts for establishing the first museum, reproduced the culture they had been exposed to in Vienna and other European cities. This is similar to the Ottoman museum, whose founding father, Osman Hamdi, was educated in Paris. Like the

DOI: 10.4324/9781003053033-4

Ottoman Museum, the Hungarian National Museum was born from the impulse of modernisation, not nationalisation. As Monika Baár (2010) suggested, back then not all the Hungarian elites were nationalist to the point of espousing separatist aspirations.

Things changed after 1867, year of the *kiegyezés* (compromise), which provided Hungary with more control over its internal affairs. The period from 1867 to WW1 and the consequent dissolution of the Austro-Hungarian Empire is marked by growing nationalist sentiments in Hungary, especially in those factions of the population that were tired of the dual rule and cultural representation (Brandow-Faller, 2011). As a consequence, great fervor arose among Hungarian national entrepreneurs researching and/or inventing exclusive Hungarian music, history, art, sport, traditions, and so on (Lajosi, 2018; Baár, 2010; Hadas, 2007; Molnar, 2007; Frigyesi, 1994). This process of inventing national traditions that contribute to imagine a unified Hungarian nation are very much in line with the theories of Eric Hobsbawm (1983) and Benedict Anderson (1991) that I discussed in the section dedicated to theory.

The most relevant neo-nationalist movement in Hungary at the turn of the century was “The Young Ones”, an expression that reflects similar nationalist movements in other countries, for example, Giuseppe Mazzini’s Young Italy, the Young Turks in Turkey, and so on. It is possible to identify these as proto-nationalist movements that would later bond with the state, taking advantage of its organisational capacity. The Young Ones opposed Westernised Hungarian institutions like the Academy of Sciences, the National Museum, and the National Theater (Alofsin, 2006), which they saw as offshoots of the Western oppressor. Poets Endre Ady, Mihály Babits, and József Kiss; painters József Rippl-Rónai, Károly Lótz, János Vaszary; ceramic producer Vilmos Zsolnay; and architects Béla Lajta, Károly Kós, and Ödön Lechner were cultural forces who espoused the nationalist cause of the Young Ones, providing it the tools for a strong ideological penetration. They struggled to find a distinctive and exclusive Hungarian style and found it in the Magyar roots of Hungary, which led them to shift from the West and turn to the East (Brandow-Faller, 2011).

This is particularly true for the Museum of Applied Arts, built in 1876. Ödön Lechner, the architect who built it, manifested the nationalist views of the group in the neo-Magyar style of the museum. This involved the use of ‘arabesques, rosettes, and majolica mosaics which simultaneously alluded to Mughal art and the stylised foliate designs of Hungarian embroidery depicted in Huszka’s work’ (Brandow-Faller, 2011: 187). The result was a patchwork of numerous different elements, including Gothic, Mughal, and British-Colonial elements that revisited traditional Magyar architecture in modern fashion.

Ethnography is central to nationalist developments in Hungarian museums. This too is similar to the Turkish museum. As in Turkey, professional ethnographic studies in Hungary started in the 19th century and attempted to define the founding elements of Hungarianness. This process demanded selectivity, and the selections 'were shaped everywhere by national interests, by ethnocentric notions of the national past and of the national future. Cultural differences from unfriendly neighbors were stressed, as were similarities to friends' (Hofer, 1990: 146). The peasant objects that Hungarian ethnographers started to systematically collect were to confirm that the selective process was based on scientific observations. In 1885, they were exhibited as part of the National Exhibition in Budapest, held in the new Ethnography Department of the National Museum. In 1896, the head of the ethnography department, János Jankó, established an Ethnographic Village modelled on the Swedish Skansen for the national Millennial Exhibition (Apor, 2011). A village of 24 peasant dwellings selected from 23 counties of the country was exhibited, showing the image of the home country's landscape to visitors.

In a relatively short time, from WW1 to the end of WW2, Hungary went through several regime changes accompanied by ideological revolutions that affected the museum institution and museum displays. These changes included the loss of 67% of Hungary's territory and 33.5% of ethnically Hungarian inhabitants (Kiraly, 2001). The first years of the interwar period were marked, as in Turkey and Croatia, by conflicts. In Hungary, these took the shape of a communist revolution led by the Hungarian Communist Party, which overthrew the Hungarian Democratic Republic established in 1918. The following counter-revolution brought what came to be known in history as the "white terror", which involved killings and deportation of communists, socialists, Jews, and leftist intellectuals.

From 1920 to 1946, Hungary was a monarchy without a king, with Charles IV, Apostolic King of Hungary, prevented from ruling by threats of war from neighboring countries and by the lack of support from Miklós Horthy, the Regent of Hungary and official representative of the Hungarian monarchy. In this period, Hungary shifted towards the far right, tying close relationships with Fascist Italy and Nazi Germany. Thanks to the German help in the interwar period, the Hungarian territory doubled, reconquering some territories lost in WW1. These included parts of Slovakia, Carpatho-Ukraine, northern Transylvania, and parts of Vojvodina.

Rising nationalism in politics had a parallel in Hungarian museums, which stressed national history as a struggle against the Ottoman-Turk and the Habsburg oppressor (Apor, 2011). Like the Ottoman museum, the Hungarian one tended to overlook the 19th century, a time of decline for the Ottomans and one of complicity with the Habsburg for the Hungarians.

The goal was to display a distinctive Hungarian nation, glorious and modern, in line with the Gellnerian principle of 'one nation in one state' (Gellner, 1983).

WW2 was a watershed. After the democratic opening to the multi-party system (1945–1948), the country turned slowly but resolutely into a satellite of the Soviet Union, and so did Hungarian museums. In 1949, a puppet government under Soviet rule inscribed all museums (and all public institutions) in a centralised system that helped to control them closely, and when needed, to exploit their space and objects. The opportunity arose first in 1949, then in 1959, when the National Museum served the communist propaganda with exhibits on the 30th and 40th anniversary of the First Soviet Republic of 1919 (Apor, 2014). Another came in 1964, when the Museum of Contemporary History was inaugurated. Its narrative emphasised the uniqueness of socialism in history. In 1967 the National Museum was rearranged for a special exhibit on "The History of Hungary since the Conquest to 1849". In this case, the objects displayed were to materialise a representation of Hungary that combined its national exclusivity within a greater Marxist framework.

This is true for several exhibitions held in communist Hungary. They would echo the pillars of communism, for example, class struggle through which interpreting Hungarian historical events. This is how ethnographic and folklore heritage in communist Hungary were used by the communists to justify their rule. An example is the exhibition for the 500th anniversary of the birth of György Dózsa. Dózsa was the leader of a peasant revolution that erupted in the central Magyar provinces in 16th-century Hungary. His fight, which targeted the aristocracy, was a perfect metaphor for communist Hungary, where the majority of the population was still employed in the agriculture sector. Dózsa's death after painful physical and psychological torture represented both the sacrifice of the Hungarian communists and the evil of their capitalist enemies. As Vukov (2011) put it, the Hungarian folklore and history were key factors in giving birth to a contemporary mass culture that held communism as its ultimate expression. Museums were the tools of transmission of that culture.

Finally, the disintegration of the USSR gave way to nationalist movements in most Soviet republics, including Hungary. The rise of nationalisms was facilitated by the relative absence of assimilation policies in the Soviet Union. This was the result of what came down to history as the Soviet version of ethnic-based federalism, which left some degree of cultural autonomy to the republics under Moscow's rule. Federalism in the Soviet Union functioned as a backdoor for nationalist entrepreneurs who based their ideology on pre-existing ethnic institutions (such as museums) in communist Hungary (Shcherbak, 2015). It wasn't long until these ethnic institutions researching and exhibiting ethnic folklore and history started to function as triggers for nationalist-separatist organisations ready to take over as soon as the Soviet Union started to crumble.

As communism brought a season of historical revisionism, so did its collapse. The fall of the Berlin wall and the end of the iron curtain marked the dismantling of the communist state, substituted with the democratic neoliberal one. All public cultural institutions, including libraries, archives, and museums, were influenced by this phenomenon. Although the policy that regulated museums in Hungary after 1989 had the goal of limiting 'state intervention into the activities of the museums in order to reshape them as non-political, public institutions, openly accessible to all members of the society' (Apor, 2012: 91), in practice it substituted the rule of Moscow with the one of Budapest. Could it be any different? Apor states that both the conservative-liberal Hungarian Democratic Forum (MDF), and the political programme of the prevalent oppositional party, the liberal-leftist Alliance of Free Democrats (SZDSZ)—that ruled Hungary alternatively until the conservative forces took over in 2010—shared the idea of radically decreasing the role of the state in managing public cultural institutions and museums. This is perhaps true on paper, but in reality, soon museums started to function as tools for constructing, rendering visible, and reviving national culture.

It is true that the transition from a communist to a democratically elected government and capitalist economy did bring more international connections, collaborations, and freedom in Hungarian museums (Vásárhelyi, 2012). This is valid especially from the 1990s until 2010, when the national-conservative party Fidesz, led by Viktor Orbán, came to power. Jenne has described Fidesz's ideology as ethnopopulism that 'combine the demagoguing of national outgroups with the demagoguing of elite' (Jenne, 2018: 549). This ideology materialises imaginary threats by 'propagating narratives whereby enemies from beyond (migrants, immigrants, ethnic minorities) couple or even conspire with enemies from above (the EU, UN, IMF, "global elites" or foreign powers) to undermine or even de-nationalize the nation-people' (Jenne, 2018: 549). For Fidesz, the answer to such threats would be the return to a mythical golden past reconstituting a more ethnically homogeneous nation and reviving traditional national values. The historical reference point for Fidesz, the era when Hungary was at its height, is the 19th century. A number of museums commissioned by Orbán's government, including the House of the Hungarian Millennium under investigation in this book, focused on this era. It is most interesting given the fact that in the 19th century Hungary was still subject to a great extent to the Austrian empire, being its economy but also culture, as mentioned above, greatly intertwined with the one of Austria.

And yet, with the coming of Orbán, the invention of a golden past in contrast with the dark present became the basis for a new legitimacy, the one of his political ideology (Pető; 2016; Jungwatanawong, 2014; Kurimay, 2016; Pytlas, 2013). Museums, as places exhibiting official representations of the past, were (and are) targets of Orbán's regime as much as they were in Erdoğan's one. A number of academic and non-academic studies which have investigated this phenomenon, focusing on new museums, exhibits, and memorials on WW2, the Holocaust, the 1956 Hungarian revolution, the communist era in Hungary, but also on the contemporary Hungarian art scene have brought evidence of this (Radonić, 2020; Jonášová, 2019; Pető, 2021; Manchin, 2015; Brait, 2015). These studies' results provide confirmatory evidence of an increasingly authoritarian regime where museums exist as institutions mirroring the party's political ideology. Jonášová (2019), Hungarian correspondent for the magazine *ArtPortal* argues that since 2013, when Orbán's administration handed the Kunsthalle (National Art Gallery) over to the Hungarian Academy of Arts (MMA)—called by many "the Shadow Ministry of Culture"—a body of self-elected conservative artists took over, predominantly men over 60 and in line with Fidesz politics. This was translated in the art that follows the directive of György Szegö, the newly appointed director: non-critical, focused on aesthetics, traditional media, local artistic production, and popularisation. As a result, in recent years, exhibits at the Kunsthalle reproduced the artistic taste of the conservative forces ruling the country, with little or no participation by women. Dominant themes were female nudes, 'shiny bums and breasts on the beach, naked women engaged in erotic scenes . . .' surrounded by phallic symbols (Jonášová, 2019). For Jonášová, these exhibits were about the old men's nostalgia for the nationalist-patriarchal order that the government attempts to bring back through its anti-LGBT, xenophobic, and misogynous policies.

Besides art museums, historical museums were also restructured or built anew. One of the most criticised is the House of Terror Museum, which exhibits state violence in Hungary by communist and fascist regimes in the 20th century. Criticism comes from a number of intellectuals claiming that the museum emphasises Hungary as a victim, overlooking evidence of the Hungarian crimes against Jews, Roma, Serbs, and political dissidents that could potentially compromise the nation's positive image (Marsovszky, 2011). As Hirschberger (2018) put it, this is recurrent in nations that, like Hungary or Poland, stood on both sides of the victim-perpetrator divide and have the tendency to construct a selective account of history that contains only favorable information about themselves. And yet, with regard to Fidesz's Hungary, the avoidance of exhibiting troublesome past events could be more than a "tendency". Orbán's administration's unambiguous sympathies for fascism are at the basis of the decision of not exhibiting or softening evidence about the collaborationist past of Hungary.

It wasn't long ago when Orbán granted the most prestigious state award in Hungary, the Order of Merit, to Fidesz party member Zsolt Bayer, a person with a long record of racist speeches, who has 'written highly provocative antisemitic and anti-Roma articles in the Hungarian media . . . referred to Jews as "stinking excrement" and has written hateful pieces about the Roma, calling them "animals" that "should not be allowed to exist"' (USHMM, 2016). Failing to recognise the connections between these events and new museums would be a mistake. In particular, it would leave a void in our understanding of how politics worms its way into museums as well as the functioning principles of the ongoing struggle between diverse political forces using museums as tools to legitimise their ideologies. This point is better explained and further corroborated by Manchin's study, which investigated the Holocaust in Hungarian museums (Manchin, 2015). The Jewish Museum, the Holocaust Memorial and Documentation Center (HDKE), and the House of Terror in Budapest are three museums reflecting different political agendas, each offering a different interpretation of the Holocaust. Without going into detail about each museum here, these case studies bring evidence about Hungary's inability to come to terms with its past and offer a clear account of some of the most important events that shook Europe's 20th century. The same occurs when other historical events are under the lens of academic investigations, such as the 1956 Hungarian revolution. Often interpreted as the Hungarian fight for freedom from tyranny, the Hungarian revolution of 1956 is an event that has reached a mythical status. All political forces attempt to associate themselves with it, each interpreting the events through different lenses. For Fidesz's other national-conservative forces, the revolution was an anti-communist struggle while for the socialists it was mainly an uprising against an oligarchic and humiliating form of rule (Csipke, 2011). Different views gave birth to different museums, monuments, and memorials like the public art installation commissioned by the socialist MSzP that was ruling in 2006, still visible in Ötvenhatosok (56ers) square, and highly criticised by the conservative right. In 2014, Orban's administration answered by placing its monument to all the victims of Hungary's German occupation in Budapest's Liberty Square. The monument materialises Hungary as the Archangel Gabriel being attacked by a German imperial eagle, whose symbolism is meant to put Hungary on the side of the victim and emphasise the role of Germany. The House of Terror Museum was meant to follow the same strategy. For Gyani (2008) this war, fought on the field of memorialisation practices, is a war for the appropriation of the past by rival remembering communities. I tend to believe that rather than communities in Hungary, the fight is between rival political parties. Clashes between communities are the result of a polarisation whose roots must be traced at a "higher" level of the political elites.

Case studies

In recent years, discussions around museums in Hungary ended up in the spotlight of Hungarian and international media. One of the most heated debates targeted the representation of the Jewish Holocaust in Hungarian museums. Especially since 2010, when Orbán's administration took over, there have been attempts, which I will substantiate here with evidence from fieldwork, to manipulate and revise the memory of the Holocaust for political purposes. At the roots of this phenomenon is nationalism, in particular, the national ideology of Fidesz, Orbán's national conservative party, which has ruled the country for over a decade. Fidesz engaged in the task of softening representations of the Holocaust that openly referred to Hungary in the interwar period and during WW2 as fascist, and as a collaborator of Nazi Germany. At the same time though, politicians within the ranks of Fidesz celebrated and commemorated historical figures who, like Cécile Tormay, were openly anti-semitic. A recent study by the Holocaust Remembrance Project, which investigated Holocaust revisionism in the EU, support this theory reporting that Fidesz government is minimising its country's participation in the genocide, rehabilitating war criminals, and introducing anti-semitic writers into the national curriculum (Echikson, 2019).

At present, there are three main institutions—with four planned for 2021—in Budapest, with permanent exhibits on the Holocaust. It's a large number when compared with Croatia's capital Zagreb, which can count on one museum far from the city center. The differences in terms of narratives between the museums are at the basis of the afore-mentioned debates. Therefore, although I focus here on the Holocaust Memorial and Documentation Center (HDKE), it is important to outline what other museums exist in the same scenario and what connections exist between these museums and Hungarian politics. Two of them—The House of Terror Museum and the House of Fates, the latter to be opened in 2021—gained particular visibility. Their detractors point to these museums as political devices to 'vilify the Communist Party and—by association—all left-of-center politicians and politics in Hungary today' (Sodaro, 2017: 60). The House of Terror opened in 2002, supported by Fidesz during Orbán's political campaign for the general elections—which he lost. Back then, this museum foreshadowed Orbán's use of cultural institutions in the years to come and Fidesz's positions with regards to historical events such as the Holocaust, the interwar period, and the communist era in Hungary.

The House of Terror equalises the Nazi and the communist eras (Radonić, 2020) but much less visibility is given to the crimes committed by the Nazi than the communist regime. The first is placed in two-and-a-half rooms out of more than 20 rooms that make up the whole exhibit, while the second has been given 16 rooms: a clear disproportion. In addition, as underlined by Blutinger (2010), the museum doesn't find any space for the crimes committed by the Hungarian regime headed by Miklós Horthy, an inconvenient past for a nationalist administration such as Orbán's, which found inspiration in Horthy's nationalist conservatism. All blame is on German-led Nazi forces, and only one room refers to the Arrow Cross led by Ferenc Szálasi, which is responsible for the deportation and mass killings of Hungarian Jews since 1944: 'this despite the fact that *at a minimum*, twice as many Hungarians were killed by the Arrow Cross than by Hungarian Communists or Soviet forces between 1949 and 1956' (Blutinger, 2010: 85).

The HDKE stands symbolically as the nemesis of the House of Terror. It points to Hungary as a Nazi collaborator and perpetrator, not a bystander, in the events of the Holocaust and does it in a way that leaves no room for doubt, bringing evidence in the form of historical data. 'It has been the first Holocaust museum in a central European post-communist country oriented toward international, "Western" role models, first of all the USHMM, one . . . relentlessly confronting the question of Hungary's share of responsibility for the Holocaust' (Radonić, 2020: 58–59). Unlike the House of Terror Museum, the HDKE extends criticism to Horthy's regime as the one that paved the way to the disasters of WW2.

Unlike the House of Terror, which is built in Andrássy Avenue, one of the most central streets of Budapest, the HDKE is far from the city center and not well advertised: 'This is one of the reasons why we don't have many Hungarian visitors. Most of them are kids who come on school trips or tourists who want to know more about Hungary's history' says M., who works at the HDKE (Interview with M.). It was built in 1999, and renovated and opened as a memorial and museum in 2004, when Hungary joined the EU. One of our interviewees, who worked at the museum installation, reported that the Holocaust memorial center was an unofficial but important requirement (Interview with A.).

With regards to the time when the HDKE was built, it's important to underline that Fidesz was the opposition. The fact that it's in a decentralised neighborhood in Budapest and poorly advertised is evidence that nationalism doesn't belong to the right and the right only. The center-left forces that ruled the country back then were reluctant to give a more central position to an institution dedicated to such a sensitive subject in Hungarian history. It turned out that, although ghettoised, or perhaps because of that, the museum turned out 'extraordinary' (Radonić, 2020).

It is possible to consider the HDKE as an institution that struggles against nationalism, while the House of Terror is the exact opposite. The first is a museum that exhibits historical evidence in the name of social justice, beyond the nation and nationalism. The second is the voice of nationalism itself. The first requires Hungarians to come to terms with their past; the second absolves them. In the House of Terror, nationalism functions as an absolving force. Its exhibit is structured to avoid spreading strong evidence of Hungary's role in the Jewish Holocaust. In doing so, the House of Terror provides grounds for and visibility to revisionist representations of the administrations supporting them with overtly encouraging resources, central locations, and impressive advertisement. Unsurprisingly, institutions that, like the HDKE, might jeopardise the legitimacy of these representations are subject to attacks. Interviews with the personnel of the HDKE corroborate this evidence.

One of the characteristics of nationalism in its extreme forms is the necessity to silence any voice that might menace the delusion meant to glorify the nation. One of the voices that needed to be silenced is that of X., an historian who worked at the HDKE. He reported in detail the pressure from Orbán's administration appointed to the museum, and his resistance. The first step here is to detail the structure in which these pressures were exercised.

The HDKE was initially funded by a non-profit institution, which explains the degree of freedom in which its exhibit was created. Later on, though, it passed into the hands of the Hungarian state and it is now funded by it. The public foundation includes a director and members of the board of trustees and political advisors. But the museum also has its own inner structure, with its director and curators, among whom is one of our informants. As a matter of fact, these two governing bodies:

> were in constant debate with each other . . . the director of the museum was a historian but the public foundation, the board of trustees and the leader of the Foundation were political . . . I and other colleagues fought for a long time against the Foundation leader who wanted to convince us to deal just with the victim side, not just the historical side, and that we should highlight also the stories of Hungarians who saved Jews. They tried to convince us to focus on these groups, saying that this was the most important part.
>
> (Interview with X)

This extract is evidence of the influence exercised by politics on institutions such as the HDKE. Politicised staff attempted to change the narrative of the museum and highlight those events that could shed good light on the Hungarian nation, counterbalancing its involvement in the Holocaust. For the historian, the politicians' requests were 'quite strange because the Holocaust is about exclusion and murder, not about the Hungarian saviors' (Interview with X.). Political advisors in the museum would suggest to historians what to research, how to research, what to exhibit and how to arrange exhibits. X. reports that the situation was surreal. Their requests were plain, without mincing words. For example, when X. and his colleagues attempted to publish a book on the Holocaust, the political advisor told them:

> Look, I don't care much about the book, the quality, the historical narrative, we're just interested in the political side of this book, you know, it's about the Holocaust. And they wanted to convince me and my co-author that the forewords should be written by a Fidesz party politician. (Interview with X.)

X. refused to go along with the politicians' request. The main exhibit wasn't changed. As a result, Orbán's administration redirected its effort towards a new museum that could mirror Fidesz's ideology. It will open in 2021: The House of Fate. In fact, the museum is already built, in the location where the railway station was that deported prisoners to Auschwitz and other concentration camps. However, it's still closed and empty inside. The reason is that it sparked criticism from Hungarian Jews and international scholars that the government is attempting to whitewash the country's role in the Holocaust. One of the ways the museum would do this is to highlight the stories of Hungarians who saved Jews, said J., who works at the Jewish Museum of Budapest (Interview with J.).

It is evident that what the government couldn't do to the HDKE, they are trying to do by building a new Holocaust memorial. The strategy here is to fund a parallel memorial center, advertise it much better than the first one, make it bigger, shinier, more visible, and starve the other by cutting its funds (Interview with X.). An important aspect in this strategy is the support from the Jewish community and professionals such as historians legitimising Fidesz's narrative. This is not always easy insofar as not all historians would risk their reputation in a politicised institution, not to mention the difficulty in convincing the Jewish community to accept the new museum. And yet, the government tried hard and succeeded.

J. reported the government's successful efforts in dividing and weakening the Jewish community. At the center of these efforts are the contacts developed between Orbán's administration and Hungarian Jews who, to improve their position in society, tied good relations with Orbán's administration. One of them is Rabbi Slomó Köves, the founder and current Executive Rabbi of the Unified Hungarian Jewish Congregation (EMIH), an affiliate of Chabad Lubavitch in Hungary, which in turn is led by Rabbi Baruch Oberlander, a protégé of Köves. Chabad is one of the world's best-known Hasidic movements, present in more than a thousand cities in the world. With Oberlander and Köves, Orbán found precious allies within the Hungarian Jewish community willing to support his projects. From the kosher slaughtering and processing, which benefits governmental subsidy, to the museum industry, the ties between Orbán's administration and EMIH also have economic reasons.

The House of Fate is one institution that falls within the relations between EMIH and Orbán's administration. In fact, the museum is funded by the government and owned by EMIH. The counterpart of EMIH in Hungary is the older Federation of Hungarian Jewish Communities, known as Mazsihisz, which strongly opposes this museum (Interview with J.). Mazsihisz represents leftist liberal Jews and it's a stronghold against Orbán's nationalism and attempt at historical revisionism. Unsurprisingly, the relations between Mazsihisz and EMIH are all but positive and as a result, the Jewish community is fractured. This is part of a divide and conquer strategy that Orbán's administration has used in other contexts such as the art community. It champions organisations that support the government and opposes the ones that don't. Orbán's recent political move, which involved the recognition of EMIH as a "highest category

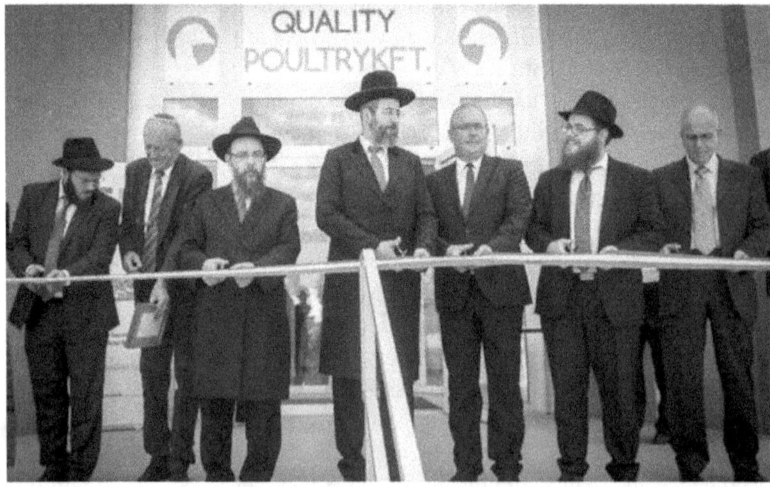

Figure 3.1 At the opening of a kosher slaughterhouse in Budapest. From left to right: Baruch Oberlander [Chabad Lubavitch], David Lau [Rabbi], Sándor Fazekas [Fidesz politician], and Slomó Köves [EMIH].

church" granted with the same state financing for educational, welfare, or cultural services as central or local government agencies, must be seen in this perspective.

The events that characterised the heated debates around institutions such as the Hungarian Academy of Arts, Hungarian Academy of Science, Kunsthalle, Ludwig Museum, the Biennale and its nemesis the OFF-Biennale, shed further light on this strategy. The Széchenyi Academy of Literature and Arts (stemmed from the Hungarian Academy of Sciences [HAS], founded in 1825) and the Hungarian Academy of Arts (HAA) are two of these institutions that became the focus of Orbán's administration. The first has a higher status as one of the branches of the prestigious Hungarian Academy of Sciences, while the second is a much younger institution born in 1992. In 2011, Orbán's government made the latter a public institution, gave it more funding, and attempted to give it the prestige of the HAS. At the same time, it gave power positions within the HAA to conservative professionals who shared his nationalist ideology. On July 2, 2019, the government ratified a law that gave the government control over a number of institutes belonging to the Hungarian Academy of Sciences. It is the same strategy used against the HDKE.

Other museums and galleries such as the Kunsthalle in Budapest were affected. The Kunsthalle, the largest institution in Budapest designed for the exhibition of contemporary art, makes for an interesting case study insofar as before Orbán's era it was recognised as one of the most progressive art institutions in Europe. The Hungarian Academy of Arts (HAA), a public body under governmental rule, took it over with a speech by president György Fekete:

> There must not be blasphemy in state-run institutions. . . . I don't give a damn about this modern democracy, for it's not modern and it's not democracy. It's not democracy, because it wants to put minority power over majority power. This is not democracy—it is anti-democracy. And in this, fascism, communism, this kind of liberalism—which I call 'pseudo-liberalism' I cannot take this into consideration.
>
> (Bajomi et al., 2020: 137)

This speech prompted a series of protests within and outside the art circles, also within the Hungarian Academy of Arts itself. The director of the Kunsthalle, Gábor Gulyás, resigned. At present, the director is George Szegő, whose manifesto included the following points:

- Art is not to criticise. Instead of tension the focus should be on aesthetics.

- Religion should not be criticised because 'there is no need to stir up tensions between the denominations'.
- Instead of "mixed-media" art, the emphasis will be on traditional techniques, in particular painting, because it has 8,000–10,000 years of tradition.
- The art gallery will hold a regular program of 19th-century "salon" exhibitions.
- The "bubble will burst" for Western contemporary art.

In 2014, Szegő criticised his predecessor Gábor Gulyás, calling him a 'leader of the small elite characterised by a lack of self-reflection' (Nolan, 2014). Mirroring Fidesz's nationalist ideology, Fekete added that there has been a lack of reverence towards the issues of nation and religion in Hungarian art. After completing his second term, Fekete, who was already over 80 years old, resigned. However, George Szegő is still the director of the Kunsthalle and he's greatly supported by the government whose funding is increasing meteorically. Vis-à-vis these developments, the director of one of the most prestigious Hungarian art institutions reported: 'we clearly underestimated the extent of the malcontent within the conservative art circle' (Interview with P.). What he meant is that Orbán's administration surfed this malcontent and gave voice to it in a way that benefited his rule. '"We wanted to be exhibited", that's what these artists said. They were the same people who, when we filled art galleries with visitors, said "Well it's good but it could be better"' (Interview with P.).

These events resulted in deep fractures within the Hungarian art field. For P., Budapest had a vivid artistic community, and small, medium-sized and big galleries such as the Kunsthalle where artists could exhibit. 'There was space for artists and a kind of path to follow, so that by exhibiting in this and that gallery would mean that they were on their way to success' (Interview with P.). The political developments of the last 10 years has changed everything. Many progressive artists 'especially in their 30s and early 40s cannot find a place to exhibit' (Interview with P.). The new nationalist conservative elite that has been given power positions won't exhibit their work. 'They are in a vacuum. . . . The only galleries that accept their work are the small private galleries. . . . They play a very important role in constructing their career' (Interview with P.).

The closure masterminded by the political institutions averse to progressive art and favoring conservative pieces links to one of the most significant protests that hit the art field in Hungary: the organisation of the OFF-Biennale. The OFF-Biennale is the largest civil, independent, and grassroots arts initiative in Hungary. For G., one of the organisers, it was

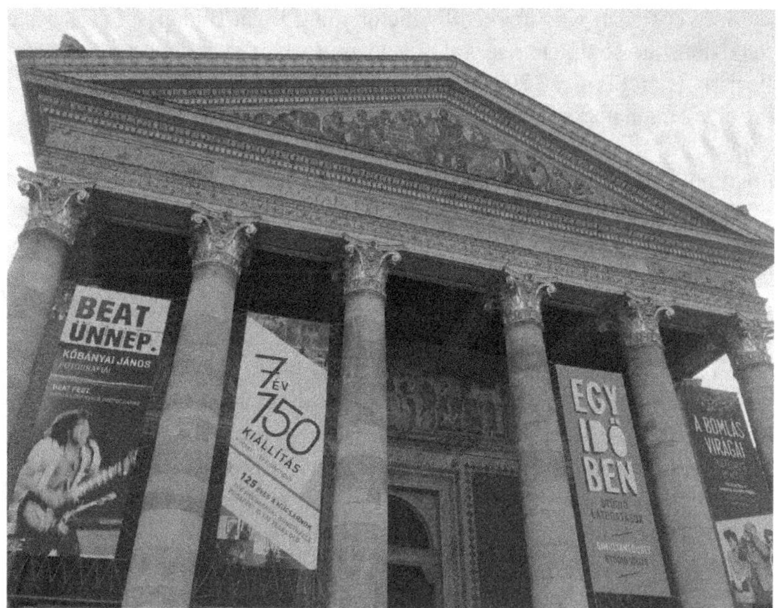

Figure 3.2 Outside the Kunsthalle.

created in 2014 with the goal of boycotting the public art infrastructure and setting the art community free from the ideological constraints of Orbán's government (Interview with G.). However, in 2021, the OFF-Biennale is in a state of fatigue worsened by the ongoing pandemic. The movement, which is self-funded, struggles to find independent, non-profit artists, independent curators, shops, houses, and other buildings where they can organise the exhibits. 'It's a huge work carried out without resources' (Interview with G.). Before the pandemic 'we met in person to decide how to organise ourselves and set strategies to resist from being obliterated by the regime. . . . Our goal was to steal the show to the Biennale. That's why we called ourselves the OFF-Biennale' (Interview with G.).

When I asked G. whether the OFF-Biennale is known beyond Budapest, he responded negatively, 'our access to the media is limited. Since 2015, Hungarian media is controlled by the state. They have five public TV channels and big funding to advertise their art scene' (Interview with G.). Besides this, reported P., head of one of the most important art institutions in Hungary, the OFF-Biennale only happens every 2 years. It has an important role as a protest against the government's power play affecting museums, but doesn't really have an impact on the lives of artists that are left out.

More criticism was sparked by the ongoing Liget Budapest Project that 'envisions the complete renewal of Budapest's largest and most iconic public park' (Liget Project, 2021). The park in question is the Városliget, one of the city's main parks. The project's goal is to redesign the park to host a new complex of five museums: the new National Gallery, new Museum of Ethnography, Transport Museum, House of Hungarian Millennium, and House of Hungarian Museum. Most of these museums are still under construction, and yet before being completed they have already been subject to criticism. The whole project is either seen by my interviewee as a great opportunity or as another political move of Orbán's administration to take possession of important cultural assets.

In our interview, P. mentioned that Laszlo Baán, the current Director of the Department of Fine Arts at the Hungarian National Gallery is also the Minister-Commissioner of this project. He is an economist on secondment to the museum industry and would represent a third way, one that differs from both the nationalist managers who rule at the Hungarian Academy of Arts and the anti-governmental art community at the roots of the OFF-Biennale. In P.'s view, the Liget Project would be the expression of a new progressive elite whose main goal is to use national (and international) art to increase profits. The logic is that the public of museums has changed. Those who were born between 1940s and 1970s are now 70 to 80 years old and are being supplanted by the new generation—a younger public born after the 1980s, now in their 30s and 40s—already earning a salary. Museums need to engage them, forge new relationships with them, and attract them, says P. The example of Baán supports this discourse. He has already re-branded the National Art Gallery in Városliget Park by hosting successful exhibits of pop(ular) artists that attracted a wide public, including the young generations. One might expect that with Baán, the project manager of the Liget Project, the new museums will follow the same profit-oriented strategy that he sees as reinvigorating the museum industry. This is what my interviewee expects. However, the fact that the new museums will be profit-oriented doesn't mean that they will be less nationalist. Indeed, the House of Terror reflects the paradigm of an institution that seeks profit using national history in a sensationalist way. Looking at the House of the Hungarian Millennium, the only one among the five new expected museums that has been completed, there are signs that this might just happen.

The House of the Hungarian Millennium is a small museum whose name echoes the 1896 Millennial Exhibition that celebrated 1,000 years since the Hungarian Conquest of the Carpathian Basin in 895. It is a museum that glorifies the history of Hungary before WW1 and attempts to link the present—thus Orbán's era—to a fictitious past almost completely overlooking the 20th century. The occasion of glorifying both pre-WW1 Hungary and Orbán's Hungary is given by the renewal of the park itself, whose project is advertised in the museum. The House of the Hungarian Millennium opened in October 2019, as Y., a guide to the museum, reported:

> The greatest celebration in the history of our people, when we celebrated 1,000-year history, we suggest that our country, the Kingdom of Hungary, was made in 896, this was the moment when we arrived here and established a new home. So, 1,000 years later, the millennium, was celebrated.
>
> (Interview with Y.)

The main attraction is a model of the park that envisages its design when the ongoing restructuring will be complete. The gate to the city park will remain Heroes Square, which is a square dedicated to:

> Our kings and heroes commemorating this 1,000-year history and amongst them, on a huge Corinthian column, stands Archangel Gabriel. Archangel Gabriel holds the double cross of the mission and the Holy crown of Hungary. Tradition holds that St. Stephen had a dream where the Archangel Gabriel appeared in this very way holding the cross of the mission and the crown and this symbol was telling him to evangelise the people. It's a symbol of a Christian and loyal Hungary.
>
> (Interview with Y.)

Kings, national heroes, and Christian-Catholic symbolism are the core points of Fidesz's national ideology: a conservative national ideology filled with religious elements that feeds on the pre-WW1 period, presented here as the golden age of Hungary. The imagination of such a glorious past gives rise to nationalistic feelings and emotions shared by Y., who reports that there was a time when 'Hungary was really rich and powerful but all was broken by WW1 and the Trianon Treaty when Hungary was amputated and lost two-thirds of the territory and one-third of the population' (Interview with Y.). For Y., WW1 was a shock 'from which Hungary never recovered, even today economy and social life, cultural life, industries still suffer from that decision in Trianon, so Orbán decided to fight the political debate in the rhetoric in the language of nationalism and national identity and that's why his main concern is to go back to the pre-WW1 era when Hungary was great and united' (Interview with Y.).

Y.'s words echo a narrative that, gestated in the interwar period with Miklos Horthy portraying Hungary as a helpless victim forced to accept Trianon, has found new life under Orbán's administration. Anniversaries of the Trianon Treaty and continuous references to Trianon are part of Fidesz's strategy to revive Miklós Horthy's far-right nationalism. In the context of the museum, these extracts are particularly important insofar as they are legitimised by an official institution for the collection and exhibition of history located in one of the most popular touristic destinations in Hungary, and beyond. This seems to be the role of the House of the Hungarian Millennium: to function as the expression of Fidesz nationalism. Fidesz xenophobia expressed in the rejection of the EU, immigrants, other religions except Christianity, LGBTQ people, and so on combines well with a narrative identifying all problems of Hungary as outside Hungary. That's why this museum represents also the endeavor of defining what is Hungarian and what is not, in particular highlighting a series of cultural elements that passes as national characteristics. These include national religion, for example, the museum presents Hungary as a distinctively Christian nation; national technology, for example, elements of modernisation such as trains and railways are represented as a national achievement; national heroes; national travellers; and national food, for example, some dishes are presented as distinctively Hungarian, such as the Gundel crêpe that is a crêpe-like variety of pancake.

Other elements are exhibited to define what is not Hungarian. One of them is communism, which is not surprising given Fidesz's political orientation. The rejection of communism as evil is represented through one of the pivotal moments in Hungarian history: the 1956 uprising against the Soviet Union that ended with a defeat for Hungary. Imre Nagy, back then the Hungarian Prime Minister, was arrested with many others, tried, sentenced to death, executed by hanging in June 1958, and buried upside-down. The narrative of the uprising has always been, since 1989 at least, at the core of struggles between the successors of Hungarian communists (The Hungarian Socialist Party) and Fidesz. The first presented the uprising as a counterrevolution against the Soviets, while Fidesz pushed to identify it as the Hungarian revolution against communism as an ideological project. The House of the Hungarian Millennium represented Fidesz's golden opportunity for marking the territory. The museum refers to the uprising and to a funeral ceremony that happened in 1989 and it was dedicated to the revolution's victims. During this ceremony, the corpses were lifted from the tombs and reburied. On this occasion, Orbán gave a radical speech against the Soviet Union, in a time when Hungary was still under communist rule and to say anything against it was seen as an act of bravery. In his speech, a young Orbán acknowledged that Imre Nagy was a communist and although he deserved respect for representing the interests of the Hungarians, communism was at the basis of his generation's failed hopes and didn't deserve gratitude (Csipke, 2011). The fact that the House of the Hungarian Millennium, built under Orbán's administration, exhibits Orbán himself and his ideological orientations can only be seen as a political use of the museum, an advertisement platform for the ruling government. It is an act of political colonisation of the museum occurring in a way that shares similarities with authoritarian regimes rather than democracies. Nationalism here is not left to chance. There is a clear design behind the goal of "selling" a certain

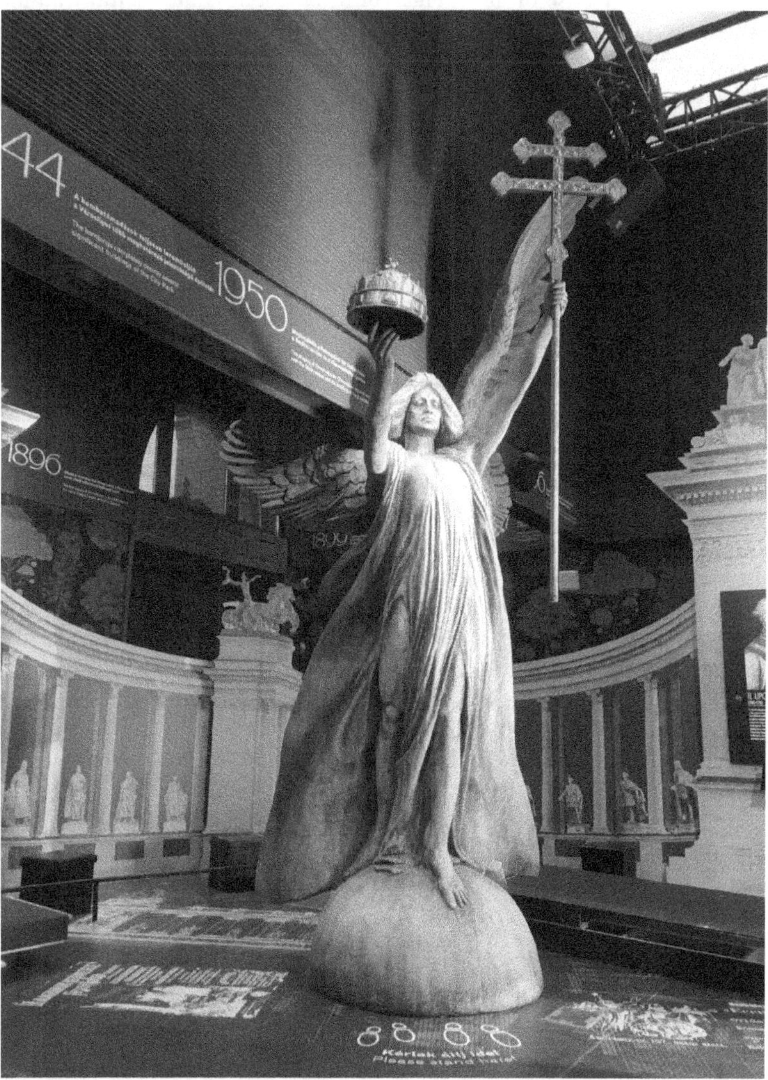

Figure 3.3 Selfie point with the Angel. House of the Hungarian Museum.

idea of the nation that matches with the one of the ruling government. The word "selling" is not coincidental insofar as the method through which the museum attempts to instill Fidesz's national vision is the same as commodity fetishism. It includes a certain use of lighting, technology, and special effects that are relatively new in the world of the museum, as they have been imported just recently from the entertainment industry. An example of this method in the House of the Hungarian Millennium is the "selfie with the Angel" corner. It is a standing point in front of a copy of the statue of Archangel Gabriel, one of the symbols of Hungary. This selfie point performs the cynical function of ideology. This function, clarified by Žižek (1994), is to avoid deepening the reasons and connections between Archangel Gabriel and the Hungarian nation—thus whether this symbol is legitimate in a country that, as any other country in the globalised world, is increasingly multicultural and multi-religious—and to actively participate (ergo the selfie) in sustaining and reproducing the conditions of the ideology.

Finally, this chapter provided material for reflection around the issue of nationalism in Hungarian museums under Fidesz's rule. It brought evidence about museums being strongly influenced by changes whose motives are attributable to nationalism, in particular, the national ideology embraced by the forces ruling the country. The influence of nationalism over the Hungarian museum was evident in the historical process of nation-making in 19th-century Hungary, and the changes occurred before and after WW1 and WW2, the communist and post-communist periods, and more recently under Viktor Orbán. The case studies under investigation opened a wider window on the ways this influence is exercised in a broad spectrum of museums, including Holocaust museums, art museums and galleries, and history museums. At the same time, these case studies showed that the influence of politicians with a nationalist agenda can be, and it was, challenged by agents who believe in and fight for a museum that is as free as possible from external influence.

4 Nationalism and museums in Turkey

This chapter focuses on nationalism and museums in Turkey. It is divided into two sections; a historical introduction to the Turkish museum from the 19th century to the present and a section on museums built under the Justice and Development Party (AKP) rule. The first section looks at historical turning points, including the birth of the museum under the Ottomans, the dissolution of the Ottoman Empire after WW1, and the museum under the Turkish Republic, until the last long rule of Recep Tayyip Erdoğan (2002–2021). The second part focuses on four case studies of museums in Turkey. Its goal is to detail how a new form of Turkish nationalism embraced by the political elites made its way through recently built museums.

The precursor of the Turkish museum is the Ottoman museum, whose development in the 19th century was one of the effects of the *Tanzimat*, the seasons of reforms. Reforms were aimed to fill the gap between the Western and Ottoman scientific and technological progress. In the 19th century, the Ottoman Empire was a modernising empire of the kind Hall and Malešević (2013) write about. Modernising empires such as the 19th-century Ottoman Empire acknowledged the existence of other powers with whom tying alliances, trade, share technology, in a few words, cooperate in a new world order. In this time, the Ottomans became increasingly interested in other empires' and nation-states' progress, so much so that Sultan Abudlaziz traveled to Europe as a modern ruler, meeting other European monarchs and heads of states, visiting European cities, taking notes on and inspiration from their progress (Palabıyık, 2016). This occurred when the Ottoman administrators acknowledged the empire's state of regression, caught between the growing power of Europe outside its borders and the rise of nationalisms within, both feasting on its vast territories.

One of the cards played to contrast growing separating sentiments was a new identity for the empire: 'one that would support shared interests with the growing powers of Europe, assure a national coherence to the empire's remaining territory, and project a shared identity for the people of the empire—

DOI: 10.4324/9781003053033-5

in short one that would transform the image of the Ottoman state from that of an empire to that of a nation' (Shaw, 1999: 57). In support of Shaw's thesis, one might say that implementing nationalist ideologies in imperial states was rather common in modernising empires, especially in those that acknowledged the dominant ideological shift marking the age of the nation-state (Hall and Malešević, 2013). This concept suits the 19th-century Ottoman Empire, which attempted to use nationalism as a tool for avoiding divisions, encouraging the variety of ethnic groups living within the Ottoman vast territory to identify themselves as Ottoman became an imperative to the Ottoman governors. The museum was one of the tools through which this was done.

Especially in its 1891 version, the artefacts, history, myths, and traditions on display at the Imperial Museum—the first museum of the empire—represented the goals of the Ottoman administration. As Shaw (2011) put it, the goal was to show the conglomeration of many ethnic groups of the Empire sharing a common past, present, and future, and a specific territory within the Ottoman state. This was fundamental also to quell separatist forces within the Ottoman's territory as they were a threat to its dominant role in the Mediterranean (Ahmad, 2008). The Ottoman museum exhibited the Ottomans as a nation, united beyond ethnic identities, loyal to the Ottoman state, and it rooted Ottoman history in the Roman and Greek civilisations. The museum came to perform two important functions: it solved (on paper) the problem of national unity, and it created a symbolic bridge with the old European enemy, with which now the Ottomans attempted to form alliances. Besides this, the museum was a sign of civilisation that entitled the Ottomans to advertise themselves as part of the civilised world, one whose path led to the development of science and technology. When considering this point, it is not surprising that the architecture of the first Ottoman museum, the Imperial Museum, resembled the one of other European museums, and its display highlighted Greek, Roman, and Byzantine artefacts. Western Europe set the dominant canon in terms of science and technology, but also culture.

The situation of museums within the Ottoman Empire didn't change until WW1, a real crossroad for the Ottoman state that ceased to exist. The heir was the Turkish Republic born from the ashes, which involved the passage from a multinational state to one that espoused a "one nation in one state" ideology. The state became Turkey and the nation the Turks. Passing from a multicultural Ottoman society to a nation-state involved a certain degree of social engineering that went down in history as Turkification. Museums were involved in it.

Turkification, initially based on ethnographic studies by sociologist Ziya Gökalp, was carried out at human cost. Rıfat Bali (1999) has described anti-Jewish measures and policies of the Kemalist regime. Turkish Jews were assimilated linguistically and were subject to economic and administrative exclusion from Turkish society. For Aktar (2000), the Kemalists targeted all non-Muslim groups in society, including Armenians, Greeks, and Jews that were identified as potential threats to the newly established Turkish nation-state (Aktar, 2000: 101–134). The Kurds, whose ethnographic studies were carried out by Gökalp himself before the fall of the empire, were thought to be highly assimilable and were soon called "Mountain Turks": Turks who lived in the mountains.

Turkish museums built in the time of Kemalism supported the governmental ideology. From the time of Kemal Atatürk, changes in the way collective memory has been constructed in museums were linked to governmental changes. As in Europe, politics played a pivotal role in Turkish museums. Under Atatürk and his legacy, museums in the 1920s–1960s had a specific focus on ethnicity, and emphasised the Turkic origins of the nation, evading emphasis on the Ottoman and Islamic past, and minorities. In the 1950s, Turkey opened to the multi-party system but Kemalism kept a strong hold on museums. In the 1960s and 1970s, the national model of museums proliferated in Turkey, whereas more important changes occurred in the 1980s, 1990s, and especially in the 2000s (Shaw, 2011). The 1980s and 1990s mark an era of privatisation of national ideology in Turkey, and an era of liberalisation and democratisation that led to the opening of several private museums built by wealthy Turkish families. Other changes occurred in the 2000s, with the rise of pro-Islamic governments led by the Justice and Development Party (AKP). Under the rule of Recep Tayyip Erdoğan, the AKP was very keen on promoting state initiatives focused largely on strengthening exhibitions that emphasised Islamic and Ottoman heritage (Shaw, 2011: 937). The works of Walton and Göktürk (2010), Bozkuş (2014), Türeli (2006), Öncü (2007, 1999), Aronsson (2011), Shaw (2007), and Bozoğlu (2020) help to make sense of this assumption.

The advent of Recep Tayyip Erdoğan was even compared to the one of Atatürk, the first President of Turkey and founder of the Turkish Republic, by Jean-François Pérouse and Nicolas Cheviron (2016) who titled their recent book *Erdoğan: New Father of Turkey?* Especially after Erdoğan's victory at the general elections of June 2018, writes Taspinar (2018), Turkey took a step toward authoritarianism. Besides, Islam entered the Turkish political arena with laws that increased the role and visibility of religion within Turkish society. To materialise the religious and authoritarian stance of Turkey's president, Erdoğan, both scholars and journalists have applied to him the epithet "New Sultan" (Cagaptay, 2017). In hindsight, the change was advertised, since the beginning of the AKP's race for power, with a popular motto, *Yeni Türkiye Yolunda* (Towards a new Turkey), which aimed to set a divide between the pre-AKP and post-AKP eras. To be new meant to be different, especially from the Kemalists, who had ruled Turkey for decades by dint of coup d'etats.

In *The Making of Modern Turkey*, Feroz Ahmad (2004) writes that there is always the thread of 'continuity which runs through the history of virtually every nation and there is rarely a total break with the past. Yet it is vital not to lose sight of the turning points' (Ahmad, 2004: 3). This is particularly important for the AKP, which although it was saluted as a new political force, was hardly a totally new phenomenon. Its ideology matched with the ones of previous parties such as Demirel's Justice Party and Özal's Motherland Party, which could be seen as Turkey's attempts at breaking free from the authoritarian rule of the Kemalists. From Özal, Erdoğan took the idea of a Turkish-Islamic Synthesis (Eligür, 2010), therefore the possibility of a political Islam in Turkey. Erdoğan has been capable of leveraging the most traditional segments of Turkish society, Islamists, who although they didn't always represent the majority of his electorate, they have always come to the rescue. An example was the failed coup d'etat in 2016, after which Erdoğan praised them in his speech announcing emergency rule 4 days after the coup attempt:

> I offer my gratitude to all those who since July 15th have filled the streets shouting their support for the state and the government. Every citizen who stood up straight against the tanks stood up against them with their faith, shouting out the *şehadet* [Muslim statement of belief].
>
> (SRGG, 2017)

In exchange, Erdoğan was always keen on maintaining good relations with the most traditional amongst his supporters. The recent reconversion of the Hagia Sophia Museum into a mosque is a gift to these segments of society, which for years had demanded to pray again in this ancient symbol of Christianism. That said, Islamism as a political card helped Erdoğan to rise to a prominent place in Turkish history. So much so that many refer to his long government as the era of Erdoğanism.[1]

Erdoğanism is the strongest political phenomenon in Turkey since Kemalism. Kemalist Turkey emphasised common roots with the West to legitimise the fact that they saw a model in it. Instead, especially after 2009, Erdoğan's new Turkey seems to build on a new national ideology, which drawing on White (2009) I call Turkish Muslim nationalism. Turkish Muslim nationalism leverages on the Ottoman, Turkic, and Islamic heritage of Turkey and much less on other likewise important heritages, such as the Greek, Roman, Byzantine, Armenian, and Kurdish.

So much so that:

> The identity of the new Turks is that of a pious Muslim Turk whose subjectivity and vision of the future is shaped by an imperial Ottoman past overlaid onto a republican framework, but divorced from the Kemalist state project. In other words, everything from lifestyle to public and foreign policy are up for reinterpretation, not necessarily according to Islamic principles (although Islamic ethics and imagery may play a role), much less Islamic law (in which few Turks have any expertise), but according to a distinctively Turkish post imperial sensibility.
>
> (White, 2009: 9)

This extract is in line with Saraçoğlu's and Demirkol's study (2015), for which the AKP has reformulated the notions of a Turkish nation, national history, and homeland. The AKP's historical point of reference is an imagined golden Ottoman past, one that carefully avoids all problematic features of this past, for example, the fact the Ottoman Empire has been a colonial force for centuries that also made use of slavery like its European counterparts (Kühn, 2007; Makdisi, 2002). Rather than being just theoretical, the party struggled to use this past with the goal of engineering a new imaginary Turk advertised through national televisions, public shows, political speeches, and as I aim to substantiate here, new museums.

Elsewhere I have written that, by functioning as cabinets exhibiting the national ideology of the ruling class, new museums sponsored by the government mirror the dream of a new Turkey (Posocco, 2020). Besides scholarly work, the debate on new museums reached the most renowned daily media in Turkey and beyond. *The Economist* (2016), *Der Spiegel* (Steinvorth, 2009), and *Al-Monitor* (Akyol, 2014) have all reported about new museums in Turkey as the result of the political changes. Both journalists and scholars have argued that the striving towards a new Turkey has become evident in newly built museums. By pointing at museums as the product of the new national ideology embraced by the government, both the academic world and the media identified an inference of the political at the expense of the cultural and the submission of the cultural for the profit of the political.

Case studies

The Istanbul Museum of the History of Science and Technology in Islam (IMSTI) is located in one of the most beautiful parks of Istanbul, Gülhane Park (Rose Garden Park). Gülhane is a wonderful cultivated green area of over 3,500 square meters, with small lakes, comfortable benches, and flowers of a thousand colours. Istanbuliots go there throughout the year, but it is in summer that this park receives most of its visits. People escape the traffic of Istanbul and the heat, and find refuge in Gülhane in the former outer garden of Topkapı Palace, one of the most important residences of the Ottoman Sultans. Within this park, along the ancient imperial walls, the IMSTI was built, in a structure which in a long-gone era hosted the stables of the Sultans.

The IMSTI opened in May 2008 and was inaugurated by the then Prime Minister Recep Tayyip Erdoğan who 'requested that the exhibition be opened during the holy month of Ramadan' (Muslim Village.com, 21/08/2010). The declared goal of the museum is to change the general view on Muslim scholars in history, in particular to emphasise their role as contributors to the Renaissance, the cultural and scientific revolution which started in Europe in the late medieval period and blossomed in the 16th century. To do so, the museum exhibition focuses on the achievements of Muslim scientists from the 9th century to the 16th century.

The first section of the museum is dedicated to scholars (the museum calls them orientalists) who were the first to acknowledge the contribution of Muslim science. As a proof of this recognition, hung on the walls are several information panels which quoted extracts from or titles of their works.

By pointing out the scientific and technological discoveries of Muslim scientists, the museum supports the thesis that Islam played a major role within the global process of scientific and technological development. In particular, by emphasising that Muslim scientists functioned as heralds of the knowledge of classical civilisations in the Middle Ages, the IMSTI claims that Islamic science and technology was the essential—although unrecognised—ingredient of Renaissance. Whether this is true or not is a matter of historical debate. Bektas and Sherman (2013) tend to support this thesis. However, what is essential to this investigation is the label of "Muslim" which the historians of the IMSTI attached to those scientists. The question is, why is there a prefix attached to science which had clear religious and political implications? Who did this? Was the scientific work of those scholars "Islamic"? Did Islamic science exist? If so, what is it, exactly?

Besides conflating science with religious and political implications, the IMSTI creates a link between Islam and modern Turkey. In particular, it names Islam as a coherent monolithic bloc—Turkey is allegedly part of it—rather than a complex of socially, religiously, culturally, and politically different regions, as it is by evidence. By avoiding the exhibition of these dichotomies within the Islamic communities, the museum ties Turkey to an imagined—in the sense of Benedict Anderson (1991)—and monolithic Islamic world. In this view, the narrative of the IMSTI could be defined as Pan-Islamic. In its political form, pan-Islamism envisages the political unity of Muslims under one Islamic state, while in its cultural form it envisages the cultural unity of all Muslims.

By presenting all Muslims as belonging to one Islam, the IMSTI functions as a cultural homogeniser of the Muslim world, yet, by claiming that "Islamic" or "Western" science exists, the IMSTI functions also as a divisive force. Bektas and Sherman (2013) argued that the IMSTI does not show science as one and universal, but links it to one or other nations with certain distinctive traits. It does this by using national and religious labels—Islamic science, Eastern science, Western science, Greek science, and so on are all expressions used in the museum—that contribute to reproduce fractures and divisions in scientific discourses. This museum doesn't exhibit science (not only at least) for science's sake but for religious and political sake, for the sake of Islam and Turkey, as is evident from the interviews with the museum personnel, bureaucrats, and politicians.

The main designer was Fuat Sezgin, a scholar who passed away a few years ago. He was based in Frankfurt, Germany, where he carried out ground-breaking studies in the field of Islamic Science. His work led him to investigate scientists living in Muslim territories from the 7th century on, and to reconstruct a great number of scientific tools they invented. These tools formed the basis of a museum in the University of Frankfurt, which functioned as a prototype for the one in Istanbul. The dynamics that brought to the construction of the latter are explained in one of his public interviews:

> In 2006, the then Minister of Culture, Mr. Atilla Koç, visited our museum in Frankfurt and expressed a desire to see another like it in

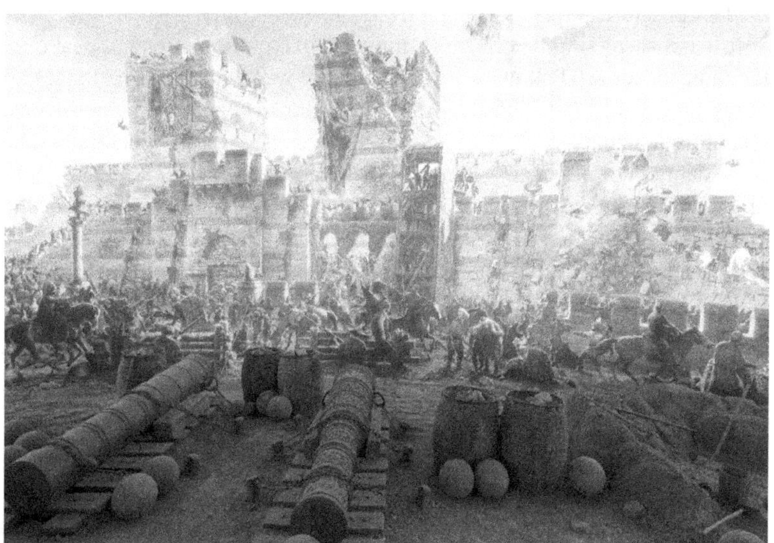

Figure 4.1 Interior of the Panorama Museum. Point of view of the visitor.

> Istanbul, which was very much my own desire as well. But at the time we weren't able to come to an agreement on how the museum would be founded. Among the visiting delegation was Mr. Muammer Güler, then the governor of Istanbul, and currently the Minister of the Interior (we have now developed a lovely friendship). As he was leaving, he lamented, "We really could have done this in Istanbul, sir. . . ." Six months later, on my summer holiday visit, I saw the imperial stables building in Gülhane Park, which had nearly finished being renovated. I was enchanted, and some friends told this to the mayor of Istanbul. A few days later, the mayor, Dr. Kadir Topbaş, visited Frankfurt, where he saw the museum and admired it very much. He called me a few days after he returned to Istanbul to inform me of the municipality's favourable decision.
>
> (Interview with Sezgin)[2]

Koç and Güler—both within the ranks of the AKP—visited Frankfurt and Sezgin's museum. They made Sezgin believe that a project to establish a similar museum in Istanbul would not be refused. Sezgin reported that he was walking in Gülhane Park when, by chance, he saw the Imperial stables almost restored. Also by chance, some friends reported Sezgin's wish to the mayor of Istanbul, who secured the agreement of the municipality to transform the ex-Imperial stables into a museum. This first important data brings evidence of the fundamental role of the politicians. Without them this museum would not exist. It was their interest, social network, and work that made it possible.

It is not surprising that Sezgin's museum exercised a strong appeal over the ranks of the AKP. It matched substantially with the AKP's national ideology and would help them to gain even more support from the diverse Islamic segments—both moderate and extremist—of its electorate. The pan-Islamic and nationalist narrative of his museum presented Turkey not only as the protector of Islam—thus reproducing a role which was of the Ottomans—but Islam as an essential part of modern Turkey. That's why relations between Sezgin and Erdoğan developed: The head of the Turkish state co-opted the intellectual whose authority could support his political statements, when the occasion occurred.[3]

The occasion occurred in November 2014, when Erdoğan stated that Muslims discovered the American continent 300 years or so before Columbus. As there is not any material proof of Muslims in America before Columbus, but just theoretical disquisitions, the international arena remained cold vis-à-vis Erdoğan's statements, whereas others mocked him. He replied, 'Those who ridicule our claim that Muslims discovered the Americas are the ones lacking self-confidence in their own history'

(Yeni Şafak, 2014). Then he added, 'This claim is not new. It is mentioned in Prof. Fuat Sezgin's books. A number of academics in Turkey and in the world have made this claim' (*Hürriyet Daily News*, 2014). Only one day after, Sezgin entered the scene and released a series of interviews in which he backed up Erdoğan's claim. The journal *Yeni Şafak* published one of them:

> The founder of the History of the Arab Islamic Sciences Institute of Frankfurt University, Professor Doctor Fuat Sezgin, confirmed Turkish President Recep Tayyip Erdoğan's claim that it was actually Muslims who discovered the Americas. . . . "As a geography historian, degrees of latitude and longitude and maps are important for me. I can say something based on these tools and evidences" [Sezgin] said and added, "I am a hundred percent sure that Muslims reached America before Columbus."

Supporting Erdoğan's statement provided benefits to Sezgin. Fatih Sultan Mehmet Vakif University created an "Institute of Fuat Sezgin" where students are taught history of Islamic science according to the principles developed by him. In addition, The Prof. Dr. Fuat Sezgin Institute for the History of Science in Islam was born. Its purpose was to:

> create a model for the institutes, departments and chairs established or to be established with the same purpose in Islamic World, and to become a center to attract students and academics. The institute at the first stage gives preference to the history of Islamic sciences, and after completing its development it aims to be interested in history of science in general. The Prof. Dr. Fuat Sezgin Institute for the History of Science İn Islam will maintain and develop the scholarly approach of Fuat Sezgin, and continuously keep alive an ambiance for the training of the historians of science of international importance.
>
> (Website of the institute)

Amongst other goals (such as providing scholarships to students who undertake studies in the history of Islamic science, etc.), the institute aimed 'to provide the museum at Gülhane Park with new objects and maintain its development . . . to endeavour to make History of Islamic Science an elective course in high schools, to put written and visual materials at the service of education'.[4] The Prof. Dr. Fuat Sezgin Institute was involved in research and teaching. Even more significantly, it had its own political agenda which aimed to make history of Islamic science an elective course in high schools. This aim was included in the constitutional reform which Erdoğan's government passed on April 16, 2017.

At the basis of this museum was a match between Sezgin's ideology and that of Erdoğan's party. Both supported the view that the 21st-century Turk had to be characterised by a higher degree of conservatism and Islamism, and that pride in the heritage of Muslims was a necessary ingredient to make it happen. Most interventions of Erdoğan's government into the private life of Turks—including telling women how many children they should have, trying to outlaw abortion and adultery, limiting alcohol consumption, outlawing coed dormitories at state universities, and more recently, quitting the EU treaty that protects women's rights—must be seen in this perspective. This museum, which supports and glorifies Islam as the religion of Turks overshadowing other religions and ethnic groups in the country, is another step towards the same nationalist project. What our data show interestingly is that politics is not enough to make it happen. It needs cultural agents such as Sezgin sharing the same ideology, the same goal, and working together towards it. The Panorama Museum 1453 is another case study bringing further evidence to this thesis.

The Panorama Museum 1453 was inaugurated on January 31, 2009 by the Prime Minister, Recep Tayyip Erdoğan, and the Mayor of Istanbul, Kadir Topbaş. The years before and after the making of the Panorama coincide with the time when the negotiations for the European membership of Turkey came to a halt, and the latter shifted towards the Middle East and the Balkans, inspired by the role that the Ottomans had played in these regions. The Panorama is better known as the museum of the conquest because it displays the siege of Constantinople by the Ottoman armies of Sultan Mehmed II, the Conqueror (Fatih Mehmed) in 1453. The conquest of Constantinople is one of the grand narratives in Turkey, which since ruling Turkey in 2002 the AKP has been keen on celebrating through conquest festivals involving state and army officials in full regalia, with ceremonial brigades dressed as Ottoman soldiers, screening movies such as Fetih 1453 on the Bosphorus, inviting huge crowds to gather for mass ceremonies on the outskirts of Istanbul, and reciting passages from the Quran. The conquest of Istanbul marks the victory of the Ottomans over the Byzantines (symbolically the victory of the East over the West), the growing expansion of the Islamic religion in the Middle East and the Balkans, and the beginning of the strong hold of the Ottomans, ancestors of the Turks.

The museum installation of the Panorama 1453 comprises a 360-degree dome equipped with spatial sounds and paintings re-elaborated through computer graphics. Visitors walk through the museum by following a prearranged path that leads them through two floors. Information panels are hung on the walls in each floor and teach visitors about the history of the conquest. On the second floor, the visitors climb a stair that rises up through a dark tunnel, which leads to the main exhibition room: the dome. The

360-degree dome displays a gigantic three-dimensional representation of the conquest. Replicas of the cannonballs used in the fight, gun carriages, and gunpowder kegs are placed everywhere to provide the visitors with the real experience of the fight. As with the Istanbul Museum of the History of Science and Technology in Islam, it is important to underline that there is nothing original in this museum. All artefacts are copies, which makes the use of the word "museum" for this building problematic. Like the Image of War Museum in Zagreb (see Chapter 5 on Croatia), the choice of using the word museum is a strategic one aimed to leverage its symbolic force and present the Panorama 1453 as an institution legitimated to represent history. Finally, special effects and spatial sounds reproduce the clashing of swords, the fire of cannons, and the shouts of soldiers. In this perspective, this museum fits with Hooper-Greehill's (1992) idea of new museums as places of entertainment. The effect is invariably powerful.

When coming to the politics of it, the Panorama 1453 shares similarities with the IMSTI. The museum was an idea of Cengiz Özdemir, Erdoğan's ex-consultant in matters of culture. Özdemir had spent years abroad, in Europe, and wanted to develop a theme park like the Madurodam in The Hague or the Mini Swiss in Zurich. These parks inspired his three projects.

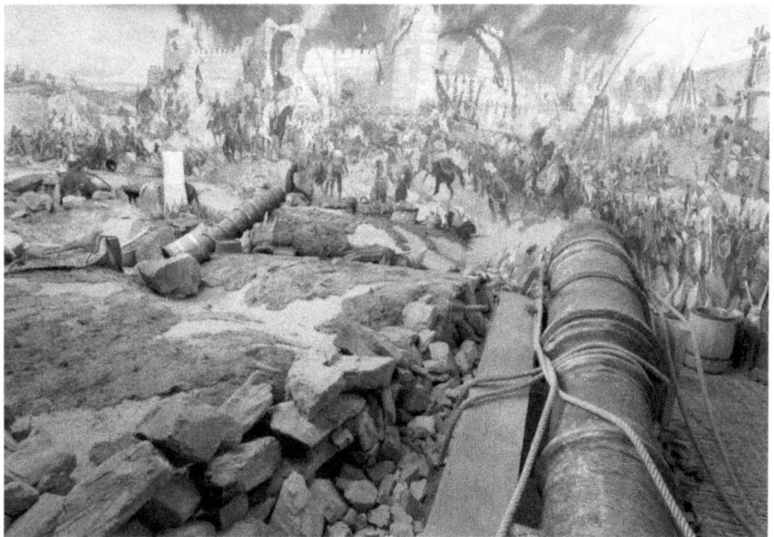

Figure 4.2 The siege of Constantinople in the Military Museum.

Source: Picture from the catalogue of the Istanbul Military Museum (2015). To be compared with Figure 4.1.

The first was the Miniatürk, a theme park in Istanbul that has been the focus of a study by Türeli (2006), the second was the Panorama 1453, and the third was a movie theatre. In our interview, Özdemir stated that the then Prime Minister Erdoğan did not agree immediately to build the Miniatürk. He could not visualise it. Yet, after some time, 'Tayyip Bey[5] called me and asked . . . "what are we going to do with this Miniatürk?" . . . He had been to Zurich and had seen the Mini Swiss theme park. Suddenly he was convinced it could be done. Decided to go on with the project, which I followed from the beginning to the end' (Interview with Özdemir).

This extract brings interesting evidence about how political decisions concerning museums are taken. Approval of the highest spheres of politics was essential to start the construction works. The same occurred with the Panorama but Özdemir left the presidency of Kültür A.Ş.—the stockholder that built and administers the museum—before the project started. Two groups, an architectural firm and a painting and special effects studio that also relied on historians as external consultants, took over and led the building. The architects created the panoramic building while the artists worked on the visual part of the museum: They planned and painted the history of the conquest on the museum dome. The latter had already had contacts with the Ministry of Culture:

> We had worked for the Ministry of Culture. A big and circular building was being built up in Topkapı. We asked them, "What is it?" and they replied, "We are building a Panorama". We asked, "Who are the painters?" They said that was to be decided. . . . We said we could do it.
> (Interview with X.)

When X. used the word "them" he referred to social capital: the artist's network of relations within the political administration. "Them" were the people the artist could contact and ask information about it. This seems like a minor detail, but it is not. The ability to reach powerful people such as the mayor or the Directorate of Construction Affairs (Imar Daire Başkanlığı) is a relevant power that grants the key to enter the circles of influential social agents in society. These connections seem to have facilitated the acquisition of the work at the Panorama. Importantly, the artists and historians were free to develop the museum. Like Sezgin at the IMSTI, the political institutions did not interfere with their job. Different sources stated that the mayor Topbaş visited the museum only once before the inauguration, complimenting the artists for their job. There was no political interference in the sense of top-down directing what kind of museum the politicians wanted. This brings evidence about the fact that these museums cannot be seen only as the product of politics, although politics plays a role in the making. Historians, artists, and architects played an equally important role. These social agents did not decide whether or not to make the museum; this decision was made by the AKP that, as Saatçioğlu (2010) stated, was always keen on supporting projects which mirrored the religious ideology of its officials and/or could back up the values of the party. But the artists were the minds and hands behind the museum. They developed the symbols, the history, the art, and in brief the whole installation of the museum, exercising a major influence over the final exhibition. The fact that they were free to develop the concept of the museum stands out as an important element that helps revise the wrong assumption that museums always reflect the national ideology of the ruling elites. Indeed, the role of the historians and artists who materially made the Panorama was capital. It is their vision of the nation, not the politicians', which entered the museum and through it was transmitted to the Turkish and non-Turkish population at large.

The case of the Kabatepe Simulation Center and Museum (KSCM) reports a different scenario, which is worth discussing here. The KSCM has been the focus of a study I wrote about more extensively elsewhere (Posocco, 2020). It's a museum focusing on the Gallipoli Campaign, in which the Ottomans and the Allies (English, French, and ANZACS, The Australian and New Zealand Army Corps) clashed between March 1915 and January 1916. This battle, which must be inscribed within the events of WW1, has shaped the Gallipoli peninsula, where the memory of the massacre is materialised in war memorials, statues, cemeteries, and museums, which have slowly accumulated over time shaping the territory [see Yilmaz (2014) and West (2010) for a wider perspective on memorialisation in Gallipoli, and Ashplant et al. (2015) for insights on the way these events shaped Australian nationalism].

The exhibit at the KSCM runs through 11 rooms that cover the history of the Gallipoli Campaign from 1914 to 1916 and its relevance for Turkey today. These events form, together with the conquest of Istanbul and the war of liberation, three grand narratives in contemporary Turkey. Although the Ottoman Empire lost WW1, Gallipoli is the one battle in which the Ottomans defeated the Allies. It represents the glory of both the Ottomans and the Turks. In addition, Mustafa Kemal Atatürk, first President of Turkey and evergreen icon of Turkish secularism, fought in Gallipoli. The KCSM represented an opportunity for framing Atatürk within the lens of Ottomanism, presenting him as one—although noteworthy—amongst many Ottomans who contribute to shape the pantheon of national heroes in contemporary Turkey. Other important figures include Seyit Onbaşı, an Ottoman soldier who during the Gallipoli Campaign loaded a missile and sunk a British vessel.[6] If Atatürk incarnates the strategic genius of Turks, Seyit Onbaşı incarnates the determination, strength, and courage. His story is often played in a theatrical setting that includes other events in the Gallipoli Campaign where the Turk inevitably wins while the enemy, in this case the British, loses.

The construction works started in 2009 and ended in July 2012, when I visited this museum the first time. The opening also saw the participation of the army and State bureaucrats, above all Recep Tayyip Erdoğan.[7] A further point in common with the Panorama 1453 is the extensive use of machinery borrowed from the entertainment industry. This includes the use of three-dimensional glasses, spatial sound, reconstruction of war fields and trenches, a pre-established path, special effects, and a narrator's voice. Videos rather than artefacts are exhibited, although at the end of the 11-room exhibition, one reaches a large exhibition area with original artefacts from WW1 and replicas.[8]

Notably, sacrifice for the nation is represented positively by the KSCM. The same message often recurs in Erdoğan's speeches. The reader may remember an event that drew international criticism, when in 2018 Erdoğan told a weeping girl that she'd receive honours if martyred (*The New York Times*, 2018). This event echoes the 10th room (there are 11 rooms in the museums dedicated to diverse events in Gallipoli), where soldier-martyrs who died for the Ottoman Empire are praised in letters dated from WW1. These letters of the fathers and mothers of dead Ottoman soldiers are read through in an emotional setting which involves music, videos, and special effects.

Like the Panorama Museum 1453 and the Istanbul Museum of the History of Science and Technology in Islam, the building of the Kabatepe Simulation Center and Museum (KSCM) was a political act. I interviewed J., one of the officials of the Ministry of Forestry and Water Affairs who took part in the construction of the museum. He reported that the idea of making the KSCM came from the general directors of the Gallipoli National Park, Veysel Eroğlu. Everything started when the Prime Minister, Recep Tayyip Erdoğan, visited the war cemeteries on March 18, 2003, the day of commemoration of the Dardanelles Sea Battles. J. reported that the Prime Minister had urged them to save the war cemeteries in Gallipoli from their state of neglect. The call was taken very seriously by Eroğlu, who administered the area until 2014. Eroğlu was a member of AKP and the man behind the building of the KSCM.

> We, as Ministry of Forestry and Water Affairs, are showing great effort in order to express our gratitude to our ancestors who gave a war of survival with their souls, blood, and all their belongings, pay tribute to the memory of our martyrs, and pass the story of The Battle of Dardanelles down to the next generations and to inform the world in the most effective and truest way.
>
> (Gallipoli Peninsula National Park. Extract from the speech of the Ministry of Forestry and Water, 2012: 5)

The words of Eroğlu echo the ones of Erdoğan:

> Without doubt, the Battle of Gallipoli, in which one of the greatest heroic legends that the world has ever witnessed was written, is not only a military victory, but also a name for a great battle of our nation won by faith and perseverance in a time of great necessity and poverty. The victory of Gallipoli has a great place in the heart of our nation not just for its being a blessed memory of our past but also for one of the strongest inspirational sources of our progress into the future.
>
> (Gallipoli Peninsula National Park, Ministry of Forestry and Water, 2012: 3)

The extracts corroborate, one more time, the thesis that nationalism played a major role in the making of these museums. The speeches of Erdoğan and Eroğlu are filled with expressions of nationalism: "Our nation won", "The victory of Gallipoli has a great place in the heart of our nation", "our ancestors", "the memory of our martyrs". These are all references to the fact that nationalism, in its versions here as Turkish Muslim Nationalism, was at the roots of the decision for building the KCSM. What came later, thus the organisation and management of the construction works are a consequence of it, although not less important in terms of turning the politicians' idea into an actual museum that matched their ideology. I interviewed some historians who worked on the scenery of the KSCM and some members of the museum's personnel, including the museum director, to investigate whether politics also controlled the process of museum building or, as in the cases of the Panorama 1453 and the Istanbul Museum of Science and Technology, didn't interfere.

E. was an historian who worked on the scenery of the KSCM. He has a PhD in history and specialised in Turkey's cultural history from the early 20th century to the present, with a particular focus on the cultural history of Çanakkale. During the interview he drew an interesting parallel between the site and museum of Troy (near Çanakkale) and the KSCM.

> When a conservative government is in charge, the narrative of the Gallipoli war prevails. When the government is liberal or leftist, Gallipoli and the war of Troy are embraced together on the grounds that both of them represent the same element: unity and resistance against the invader. . . . Attempting to emphasise this, some have called the Gallipoli war the last Trojan war.
>
> (Interview with E.)

What E. meant is that pro-Islamist governments such as the AKP tend to emphasise Gallipoli because it represents the last successful battle fought by the Ottoman Empire. Gallipoli lends itself well to both nationalism and religion insofar as modern Turkey can be identified as the heir of the Ottomans. Instead, the fact that Troy was a classical civilisation that shared cultural elements with ancient Greeks makes it more attractive to Kemalists and less to neo-Ottomanists, although in both cases the main theme is the attack by foreign forces and the invasion of (today's) Turkish soil. The invasion discourse was also very much present in the KSCM and was supported by the Turkish historians who prepared the museum exhibition. I interviewed six of them and all emphasised the fact that Gallipoli represents an invasion which had been planned long before WW1. Without using the word "conspiracy", they supported the theory that Western powers plotted against the Ottoman Empire. E. put it in the following terms:

> There is an Ottoman Empire which is doomed to collapse whatever happens. . . . On the one side there is a group led by England, on the other side there is Germany and the Austro-Hungarian Empire. Both groups want to pull down the Ottoman Empire. . . . Death is certain! The Ottoman Empire shall collapse, it does not matter how the war ends.
>
> (Interview with E.)

It is particularly interesting how E. combined facts and interpretation of facts to assert—without hesitation—that the Ottoman Empire was the target of a conspiracy. What is central here is not whether E. is right or wrong but that he holds a position which is one of many positions concerning the history of the Gallipoli campaign. In fact, there are other historians such as Feroz Ahmad, known for his *Making of Modern Turkey* (2004 [1991]), who stated that rather than the result of a conspiracy the dismemberment of the Ottoman Empire was the ineluctable consequence of its archaic political and social system. He said 'the end of the Ottoman Empire ought not to be any cause for surprise; the puzzle is that it survived as long as it did' (Ahmad, 1984: 5). Acknowledging different point of views is vital here insofar as it is through the making of the museum and the spreading of its narrative that the position of E. becomes the dominant position.

The same point of view as E. was held by other historians who worked for the KSCM. All of them emphasised the fact that Europeans had planned the dismemberment of the Empire. The commonality of views is interesting, in particular because the Turkish historians agreed between them and their view matched with the view of the political administrators who hired them. I wondered whether this was a pure coincidence or politics somehow exercised control over the museum. Asking more questions about the way the committee decided what information should be included or excluded I discovered that when the historians suggested to include events that moved away from an ever positive representation of Turkey, they were not included in the final exhibit.

One of these events is the attack on the port of Odessa (Russia) ordered by Enver Pasha (Minister of War of the Ottoman Empire) on October 29, 1914 (Tucker, 1996: 174). Enver's act caused the cascade of events which brought about the declaration of war by Russia and its allies on the Ottoman Empire. This information was not included because it would have put the Ottomans in a problematic position, suggesting that it was them who started hostilities, not the Allies and their secret agenda. When I asked E. why this information is missing, he reported that the events of Odessa had been initially included but were removed at a later stage because they involved too much detail which would otherwise annoy the visitor. This first element suggests that historical truthfulness was subject to the degree of satisfaction of the public. Instead, M., another historian who worked at the KSCM, provided a different answer. Here is an extract from the interview:

M: States do not want to say things to the detriment of themselves.

Interviewer: What do you mean exactly when you use the word "State"?

M: The people around the [museum] directors, the Prime Minister and the President; their consultants.

Interviewer: Why isn't there any reaction from the historians?

M: If politicians ignore their opinions what can they do? Protest? No! We have no power . . . in the academia nobody feels free to say what they think. You can only talk in accordance with the present government. If you disagree you may be labelled as a traitor. We cannot live in harmony and academicians cannot talk freely.

Interviewer: There was a council of experts and there were historians—you were one of them—who signed documents and by signing them, approved the exhibition plan.

M: In those things there is no professional approach. Probably people sign for the sake of relationship. One may not be able to say no. They hope to make up the mistakes later, therefore they sign.

(Interview with M.)

This extract proves that politicians did not have an interest in showing historical events which could cast a shadow on the national past, which therefore were excluded. How did this materially happen? M. stated that the committee would provide "Ankara" with proposals of events to include in the museum exhibit and "they" would either approve or disapprove. When disapproved, events were left out.

For the sake of clarity, there are other studies supporting this view. Not long ago Shaw (2011) wrote that Turkey's museums are implicitly understood as places of positive representation where particular narratives are celebrated. For Shaw, Turkish museums are not places of collective critique but spaces 'defined by a classical hegemonic paradigm where the narrativisation of collective identity production is top-down, and thus is either informed by the state or by elite private actors often closely affiliated with it' (Shaw, 2011: 943). This view matches with M.'s, whose extracts provide insights into the way the classical hegemonic paradigm is materially implemented.

The fourth and last case study, the Istanbul Military Museum, doesn't add much to the way nationalism enters Turkish museums but provides details about the substantial coherence of national narratives within them. Different national ideologies influence museums' exhibits but some narratives change only superficially, no matter if a progressive or a conservative government rules the country and/or sponsored the museum. One might call these narratives "grand narratives" (Ross, 1995) or "master narratives" (Megill, 1995) that involve the story of a people as a nation. These are 'necessarily a mythic construction' (Ross, 1995: 653) whose many versions aren't but the further confirmation that that nation exists and has peculiar characteristics that identify it amongst other nations, including a (often glorious) national past and a future. Through the investigation of the Istanbul Military Museum, which is administrated by the Turkish army—which is historically the stronghold of Kemalism and therefore ideologically at the polar opposite of the AKP—I will attempt to substantiate this assumption.

This museum is located in Harbiye, a district whose name comes from the Arabic word *Harb*: war. It was founded in 1950, although part of its collections—mainly military spolia and trophies of war—were exhibited, since 1846, in the ex church of St. Irene. Its focus is rather wide, comprising around a thousand years of history of war, including weapons, uniforms, and all those objects in use by the military. It exhibits the siege of Constantinople and the Gallipoli Campaign that are also the narrative of the Panorama Museum 1453 and the Kabatepe Simulation Center and Museum (KSCM). The main difference between the Panorama Museum and the KSCM on the one side, and the Istanbul Military Museum, on the other, is the use of technology to elicit a deeper emotional response in the visitor. The Istanbul Military Museum is more a traditional museum than a place for entertainment. In terms of national narrative though these museums share many similarities, although they have been built by political forces—AKP and

CHP (Republican's People Party)—whose national ideologies, on paper at least, do not share much.

Both the siege of Constantinople exhibited by the Panorama Museum and the Military Museum represent the Ottoman ancestor in the act of conquering the city, soldiers wave the Ottoman flag under the command of Sultan Fetih who, on his horse, orders the attack. In both museums, reproductions of weapons, armors, and fences combine to give a sense of realism. The goal is clearly to show the Turkish ancestor as a powerful and victorious conqueror.

Representations of Turkey as a nation of warriors recur in different forms in these museums. In an interview with the manager of the Panorama 1453, he said 'Do you know why we have so many museums? Because we won many wars' (Interview with Y.). The "we" Y. refers to entails both Ottomans and Turks as one national community. In his mind, Ottoman victories are Turkish victories and together substantiate the view that Turkey is a warrior nation that fought for and conquered the fatherland (*Vatan*). In this narrative the nation is both the beginning and the end of a project whose tones are almost mystical, as the words of Atatürk, chosen as forewords of the catalogue of the museum, suggest: 'That is the Turk: lighting, storm, the sun which illuminates the world' (Catalogue of the Military Museum, 2015: 29). The same national project assumes more religious features in the Panorama Museum 1453, whose silhouette of Sultan Fatih (conqueror of Constantinople) is embedded in the clouds. Yet, their goal is the same, to glorify the Turkish nation.

Also, the narrative of the Gallipoli Campaign in the Military Museum (Çanakkale Savaşları Salonu) shares similarities with the one exhibited by the KSCM. Both emphasise the efforts made by the nation to push away the invader and preserve national-territorial unity. Like the KSCM, also the Military Museum transmits the idea of the Ottoman Empire as a victim. This concept is represented by a massive explosion hitting the Turkish troops. The scene in question shows wounded soldiers in the act of being medicated, representing both the sacrifice of and for the nation, and national brotherhood. Interestingly, when the attacker is the Ottoman ancestor, such as in the Panorama Museum 1453 or in the KSCM when Seyit Onbaşı sunk the Allies' vessel, the scene is represented in a way to symbolise courage, spirit of sacrifice, and justice. These events function as a kind of coherent set of narrative elements on which diverse political forces can draw, giving body to their national ideology. In this perspective, it is not surprising that some heroes staged by the AKP, such as Seyit Onbaşı, are heroes also in museums built by the CHP. This confirms the fact that one of the most important features of ideology—in this case nationalism—is its versatility (Žižek, 1994).

The core discourse here is that these museums represent war in a way to preserve an ever-positive representation of the nation. They do it by manipulating historical events, thus overlooking certain details or presenting them in a way that improves or at least doesn't go to the detriment of the nation. However, in some cases they push themselves further, reaching a level of manufacture that goes under the term of historical negationism or denialism that is performed by willingly falsifying and therefore distorting historical records. As a case study, I focus on a temporary exhibit on the 1974 war in Cyprus that I visited in 2016 during a fieldwork in Turkey.

Greeks call this war "Turkish Invasion of Cyprus" while Turks call it "Cyprus Peace Operation". It began when the Turkish army attacked Cyprus after the military junta in Greece performed a coup d'etat to depose Cypriot president Archbishop Makarios III and installed a puppet government led by Nikos Sampson. For the sake of clarity, the 1974 events have their roots in a turbulent history of clashes between Greek Cypriots and Turkish Cypriots that goes back to the 19th century. Both parts claim Cyprus as their national territory, each bringing evidences that benefit their side while going to the detriment of the other. Although I focus here on the Istanbul Military Museum, there are other museums in Greece and South-Cyprus that perform the same role as nationalist cabinets (Bounia and Stylianou-Lambert, 2011). What is worth mentioning is that historically both sides have resorted to violence towards civilians, including children, women, and the elderly, using terrorist methods such as kidnapping, summary executions, torture, and so on, and yet both exhibit the war by emphasising their role as victims, not perpetrators, in an endless circle of accusations whose only result is increasing tensions between the two countries.

With regards to the exhibit at the Istanbul Military Museum, it exhibits exclusively on the crimes committed by Greek Cypriots and commemorates only Turkish victims. The exhibit goes all the way from ancient history to the foundation of the Turkish Republic of North Cyprus attempting to substantiate the idea that 'Cyprus was never entirely ruled by Greeks in history nor became a Hellenic Island' (Leaflet of the Exhibition at 41st anniversary).

The leaflet of the 41st exhibition mentions that 'Muslim Turks and Orthodox Greek Cypriots *lived in peace and harmony* as two different national communities *until 1821 under the structure of "millet (communal) system"*[9] of the Ottoman Empire' (Leaflet of Cyprus Peace Operations, 2015). According to this version of history, Greek Cypriots are to blame for worsening the relations with Turkish Cypriots. British colonialism, in particular the establishment of a British protectorate on Cyprus, further worsened the situation until EOKA (*Ethniki Organosis Kyprion Agoniston*, National Organisation

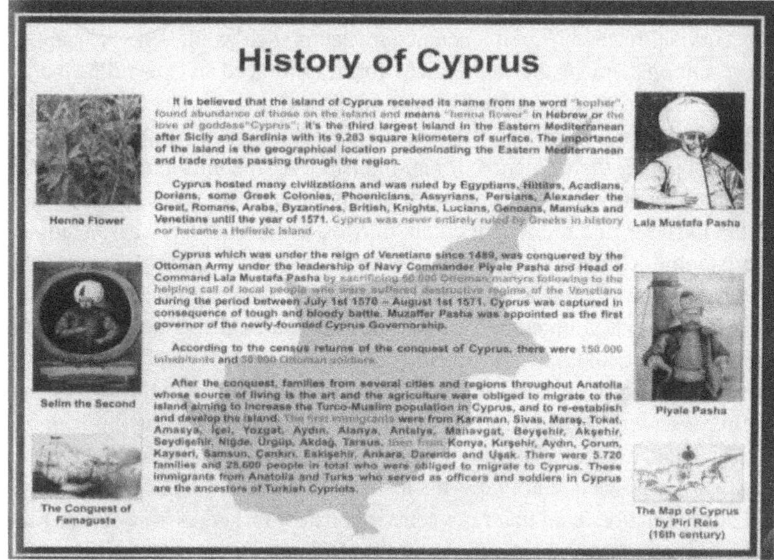

History of Cyprus

It is believed that the island of Cyprus received its name from the word "kopher", found abundance of those on the island and means "henna flower" in Hebrew or the love of goddess"Cyprus"; It's the third largest island in the Eastern Mediterranean after Sicily and Sardinia with its 9.283 square kilometers of surface. The importance of the island is the geographical location predominating the Eastern Mediterranean and trade routes passing through the region.

Cyprus hosted many civilizations and was ruled by Egyptians, Hittites, Acadians, Dorians, some Greek Colonies, Phoenicians, Assyrians, Persians, Alexander the Great, Romans, Arabs, Byzantines, British, Knights, Lucians, Genoans, Mamluks and Venetians until the year of 1571. Cyprus was never entirely ruled by Greeks in history nor became a Hellenic island.

Cyprus which was under the reign of Venetians since 1489, was conquered by the Ottoman Army under the leadership of Navy Commander Piyale Pasha and Head of Command Lala Mustafa Pasha by sacrificing 50.000 Ottoman martyrs following to the helping call of local people who were suffered destructive regime of the Venetians during the period between July 1st 1570 – August 1st 1571. Cyprus was captured in consequence of tough and bloody battle. Muzaffer Pasha was appointed as the first governor of the newly-founded Cyprus Governorship.

According to the census returns of the conquest of Cyprus, there were 150.000 inhabitants and 30.000 Ottoman soldiers.

After the conquest, families from several cities and regions throughout Anatolia whose source of living is the art and the agriculture were obliged to migrate to the island aiming to increase the Turco-Muslim population in Cyprus, and to re-establish and develop the island. The first immigrants were from Karaman, Sivas, Maraş, Tokat, Amasya, İçel, Yozgat, Aydın, Alanya, Antalya, Manavgat, Beyşehir, Akşehir, Seydişehir, Niğde, Ürgüp, Akdağ, Tarsus, then from Konya, Kırşehir, Aydın, Çorum, Kayseri, Samsun, Çankırı, Eskişehir, Ankara, Darende and Uşak. There were 5.720 families and 25.600 people in total who were obliged to migrate to Cyprus. These immigrants from Anatolia and Turks who served as officers and soldiers in Cyprus are the ancestors of Turkish Cypriots.

Henna Flower

Lala Mustafa Pasha

Selim the Second

Piyale Pasha

The Conquest of Famagusta

The Map of Cyprus by Piri Reis (16th century)

Figure 4.3 Leaflet of the Cyprus Peace Operation. History of Cyprus.

of Cypriot Fighters) started hostilities in 1955. The museum identifies them as terrorists, while the TMT (*Türk Mukavemet Teşkilatı*, Turkish Resistance Association), the Turkish equivalent of EOKA, is described as an organisation that operated in 'great discretion and defended the possessions, lives, the pride, the honor, the dignity, the homeland, and the freedom by sacrificing everything under the tough conditions, attacks, pressures, and every lawless murder against Turkish community committed by EOKA' (Leaflet of the Cyprus Peace Operation).

Indeed, evidence proving that TMT was as a terrorist organisation as EOKA is borne out by a consistent body of studies (Navaro Yashin, 2009; Yennaris, 2003; Uludağ, 2004) that the exhibit doesn't consider. The museum reports the number of Turkish Cypriots who died, but not the number of Greek Cypriots, to support the idea that the Cyprus Peace Operation in 1974 was indeed aimed to 'honourably serve the humanity and the world peace' (Leaflet of the Cyprus Peace Operation). The exhibit ends with information about the foundation of the Turkish Republic of North Cyprus and its counterpart the Republic of Cyprus (which is not recognised by Turkey as such; the Turkish government calls it Southern Cyprus Greek Regime).

Finally, the data yielded by the case studies investigated here provides convincing evidence that nationalism was, and still is, a force shaping the Turkish museum. Even a science museum such as the IMSTI is apt to serve nationalism in the ideological form, embraced by the ruling party, whose success seems granted by the support of experts, as Smith (2006) calls historians and other professionals in the museum. Rather than just acknowledging the influence of nationalism over the museum, this chapter attempted to provide details about the many forms that nationalism can take in the museum and the way it enters it. Most importantly, the case study of the Istanbul Military Museum helped to shed light on the influence of the AKP, Turkish Muslim Nationalism, on the landscape of museums in Turkey. Rather than a unicum, Turkish Muslim Nationalism seems to be one among other ideologies, perhaps the last chronologically, including Kemalism, which left their mark on the Turkish museum. Indeed, the analysis of the representations of historical events exhibited by museums built under the AKP and museums built before the AKP seem to share more than one is ready to acknowledge at first. This leads to the question of a deep ideological core of nationalism that represents a constant in Turkey since its institutionalisation when the Turkish Republic was born. Perhaps performing their role, Erdoğanism and Kemalism scratch just the surface of this core. They might dictate the characteristics that a Turk should possess in order to be part of the nation, therefore excluding those who do not possess them. They might project Turkey towards a specific future or highlight the past, and yet they never question the existence of the nation. In this perspective, the Turkish museum, which shares many similarities with the Hungarian and Croatian museum, might be just another product of nationalism, an institution that gives body to, reproduces, and legitimises the existence of a nation that is first and foremost imagined, just an idea in the minds of people. An idea that carries profoundly real consequences.

Notes

1 For an advertisement for the celebration of the Conquest of Istanbul by Sultan Fatih, supported by the Municipality of Istanbul and the Presidency of the Republic of Turkey, copy-paste the following link in your internet browser: www.youtube.com/watch?v=5dxg5mkoswc (Last accessed on 1/29/2019)

2 The interview appears on the online platform Skylife.com at www.skylife.com/en/2013-11/the-istanbul-museum-of-the-history-of-science-and-technology-in-islam (Last accessed on 4/11/2021)

3 For a picture of the meeting between Erdoğan and Sezgin please visit www.tccb.gov.tr/en/news/542/53656/president-erdogan-receives-prof-fuat-sezgin (Last accessed on 4/23/2021)

4 For the Fuat Sezgin Sezgin Institute please copy-paste the following link https://en.ibtav.org/ Particularly interesting are the various pictures where Sezgin introduces

the visitor to his goal: 'to introduce the truths of Islamic Science to people belonging to the Islamic community, to save them from wrong judgements that negatively affect their self-esteem, and to bring them to their belief in the creativity of the individual'.

5 The use of the expression Tayyip Bey indicates familiarity between Özdemir and Erdoğan. Bey represents here the informal way of addressing the Prime Minister.

6 The full video of Sehit Onbaşı can be seen on the following link: www.youtube.com/watch?v=X9z-Sq1UyJw (Last accessed 3/22/2021)

7 For a picture of the event please visit www.canakkaleili.com/canakkale-destani-tanitim-merkezi.html (Last accessed on 4/23/2021)

8 Video showing the emotional setting in which the visitor is immersed when visiting the KSCM is freely accessible at www.youtube.com/watch?v=DGI5kKBCBpU. English subtitles. (Last accessed on 3/22/2021)

9 Original emphasis

5 Nationalism and museums in Croatia

This chapter focuses on the relationships between nationalism and the museum in Croatia. The first section covers the history of the Croatian museum from when Croatia was a region under the rule of Austria-Hungary to the creation of the present Croatian nation-state, officially the Republic of Croatia. The second section is more focused on recent museums and its goal is to deepen our understanding of how nationalism worms its way through the museum and the influence it exercises. A number of case studies of museums in Croatia, including the in-depth investigation of the Jasenovac Memorial Site Museum, the Image of War Museum, and the 80s Museum will serve this purpose.

Like Turkish and Hungarian museums, the Croatian museum also was born in the age of empires. In 1821, when the first museum—the Archaeological Museum of Split—was built, the region of present Croatia was under the rule of Austria-Hungary. The decision of constructing the museum came from the Austrian Emperor Franz Joseph I himself, who had visited the region and ordered it to collect and exhibit the archaeological evidence of the Roman past. As in Turkey and Hungary, the beginnings of the museum in Croatia are attributable to a top-down process headed and coordinated by the ruling class (Lukic, 2011: 151). Besides the Archaeological Museum of Split, another museum, the National Museum of Croatia, came to light in 1833. This time not the Austro-Hungarians but an elite group of Croatian intellectuals—the Illyrian Renewal Movement (1830–1848)—headed the construction works. The goal was to exhibit and strengthen a sense of Croatian nationalism that lies at the basis of a process of nation-building in Croatia. As in Hungary and the Ottoman Empire, also in Croatia intellectuals played an important role in this process. There was great fervor among intellectual circles for imagining and/or inventing Croatia as a nation, canonising its language, music, and traditions, researching its history, art, and sports, and finding suitable places to exhibit it. The museum was one of the legitimising showcases of the nation.

DOI: 10.4324/9781003053033-6

It is not surprising that Emperor Franz Joseph didn't look favorably on the new national museum. Its existence materialised the specter of insurrections that, like the French revolution, ended with headless monarchs. This is the reason Austria-Hungary didn't officially recognise the National Museum until 1866, 30 years after its construction. Unsurprisingly, change came at a time when the Austrians accepted the idea of providing its satellite countries with more political freedom. Soon, more museums followed. The Croatian Natural History Museum was built in 1866; the Museum of Arts and Crafts was built in 1880 and 'served to prove distinct Croatian culture and talent . . . to construct common multinational culture with the imperial center and other nationalities of the Monarchy' (Vranić, 2016: 1); the Strossmayer Gallery of Old Masters was built in 1884 'to enlarge the scope of Croatian cultural tradition through the appropriation of European élite culture' (Dulibić and Pasini Tržec, 2016: 614). These museums and galleries represent the first of their kind in Croatia. Many still exist and exhibit in the present, although the passage of time transformed them to the roots. The turmoils of history—in particular two world wars, the Communist era, and the recent phase of democratisation and liberalisation—forced them to adapt and change.

The dissolution of Austria-Hungary was one of these pivotal moments. After WW1, Croatia became part of the Kingdom of Serbs, Croats and Slovenes, the forerunner of Yugoslavia. In 1919, the Ethnographic Museum of Zagreb saw the light. As in Hungary, the ethnographic museum in Croatia was meant to exhibit—and therefore give body to—a new Croatian nation whose identity was intertwined with the supra-national pan-slavic one. Unlike in Hungary though, artefacts exhibited by the Ethnographic museum underlined the proximity between Croats, Serbs, and Slovenes in terms of culture, shared past, and future (Bonifačić, 1996). This was done to unify, as it happened in 1929, the three national groups under one supra-national community: the Kingdom of Yugoslavia. The latter lasted, not without convulsion, until 1941 when the Axis powers invaded it, divided its territories between Germany, Italy, Hungary, and Bulgaria, and allowed the creation of an Independent State of Croatia (*Nezavisna Država Hrvatska*, NDH): an Italian-German quasi-protectorate. This period, which goes from 1941 to the end of WW2 is one of the most contested in Croatian history, in particular because the Italian-German coalition favoured the Ustaša's regime. This was the Croatian counterpart of fascist Italy and Nazi Germany and reproduced these regimes' ideologies in a distinctive Croatian way, targeting Serbs, Jews, Roma, and Croatian political dissidents. As I will point out, concentration camps built in Croatia, among which one of the biggest is in Jasenovac (South of Zagreb), are still at the center of heated debates in many spheres of Croatian society, including museums.

The end of WW2 left Yugoslavia in the hands of General Josip Broz Tito's communist partisans. Tito's Yugoslavia is best known as the "third way", as he was attempting to move from both China's and the Soviet Union's models, combining communism with some elements of capitalist economy. This was the end of the Independent State of Croatia, the royal rulers were deposed, the monarchy was abolished by the Yugoslavian Communist Constituent Assembly, and the Democratic Federal Yugoslavia came into essence. As soon as the communist propaganda machine functioned, the Museum of the Revolution was built (this was later named the Museum of the Revolution of the People of Croatia). Its goals were the same as other museums of the revolution built in all the satellite countries of the Soviet Union, together with Stalin's gigantic statues, squares, and cemeteries dedicated to communist heroes. They were to glorify communism and rewrite the history of Croats through the lens of class struggle. Another goal was to reinforce 'the legitimacy of the socialist state by exhibiting and narrating the local history and culture of a region within the larger trajectory of socialist Yugoslavism' (Palhegyi, 2018: 17). These museums presented the victory of each communist revolution as truly Hungarian, Croat, Romanian, Bulgarian, Czechoslovakian, and so on. In particular, the Croatian one focused on the naturalness with which the people joined the Partizan Army, presenting 'the contribution of the people of Croatia in the general struggle of the peoples of Yugoslavia in national revolution' (Ščukanec, 1957: 3). Unsurprisingly, any reference to the aid that the Allies, especially the British, American, and the Yugoslavian royal government (in exile in the UK), provided to the Kingdom of Yugoslavia to fight the Axis was deliberately concealed. Museums were led as instruments of propaganda: to educate the masses on the principles of communism. Nothing was left to chance; even the architecture of the museums and the buildings' previous history was important, as it is proved by the museum of the revolution in Zagreb. This museum was first designed as a Salon of Fine Art to the glory of Yugoslavia's King in 1938. From 1949 to 1955 it was turned into the Museum of the Liberation; later on it became the Museum of the Revolution and, finally, the Museum of the Revolution of the people of Croatia (Lukic, 2011). The message was obvious; the Soviet Union was trying to erase the memory of the monarchy and replace it with the socialist one.

Not only were new museums built to spread the new political ideology, but old ones were restructured to match it. The National Museum of Croatia was one of these. It became the Historical Museum of Croatia and revisited Croatian national myths through socialist Yugoslav lenses. History had a special role in communist satellites such as Croatia where it provided historical continuity to class struggle and presented communism as the just culmination of centuries of injustice. For many, and certainly for communist Yugoslavians, nationalism became a matter of secondary importance vis-à-vis the promises of the revolution. This change in attitude was functional to the unity of a people, the Yugoslavians, formed by many ethnic groups and religions. As Palhegyi (2017) put it, 'This reorientation positioned already known and celebrated, albeit not overtly nationalist, Croatian figures within a specifically Yugoslav framework, recognising their specific national merits while re-narrating them as evidence of the historical precedents of socialist Yugoslavism' (Palhegyi, 2017: 8). It is worth mentioning that, as Malešević put it, socialist Yugoslavia was averse—and understandingly so—to ethnic nationalism but was still nationalist itself. Its goal was to integrate, like the Ottomans, different ethno-national projects within the Yugoslav supranational one based on civic nationalism (Malešević, 2002).

The fall of the Berlin wall and the end of communism was a crossroad in Croatia which, seeking independence from the Socialist Federal Republic of Yugoslavia, was attacked by the Serb-controlled Yugoslav People's Army. A traumatic civil war began with losses on both sides and consequences still clear in the relationships between the Serbian and Croatian states. In 1995, when the war ended, Croatia was an independent nation-state recognised by the international community, ready to embark on a new process of nation-building. It's surprising that, like several other post-communist states, including Hungary, also in Croatia the pre-communist period is perceived as the golden era (Radonić, 2011). Museums built under communism were destroyed or "renovated", exhibits were dismantled and dismembered, and their artefacts were moved to enrich other museums' collections. The extent of this destruction during and after the war suggests that Yugoslavia has been killed more than once: a first time in 1991 with its dissolution, and many other times when its memory in monuments, memorials, and museums was targeted and destroyed. It will suffice saying here that as once part of the Republic of Yugoslavia, most of these constructions were to remember what the Soviets (and Tito with them) called the National Liberation War, the war against fascism and nazism. In hindsight it's not surprising that these monuments were turned into piles of rubble. They constituted the visible proof of Yugoslav identity and therefore were subject to *damnatio memoriae*.

After the war, one problem that the new Croatia had to deal with was if and how to exhibit problematic historical events such as the collaborationist period, the communist era, and the more recent civil war.

Criticism towards the Ustaše started only in the 2000s, when the country's main goal was to join the EU. Before, little or nothing was done in museums to exhibit about death camps that operated in April 1941 (Mataušić, 2003; Goldstein and Goldstein, 2016). Franjo Tuđman, first president of Croatia and leader of a coalition of social democrats and liberals, sparked criticism for his plan of building a memorial area in Jasenovac whose goal was to commemorate both Ustaše's victims and Ustaše killed by partisans. In Tuđman's mind, the memorial was to equate fascism and communism, presenting them as two evils, and Croatia their victim (Radonić, 2011). That Tuđman, an ex-partisan, advertised such a project says much about the strength of Croatian nationalism, an ideology that Croatian partisans felt strong as much as their fascist counterparts. It tells much also about the resurgence of the far-right fringes of Croatian nationalism since the very first phases of Croatia's independence. Groups within the Croatian Defence Forces who were inspired by the Ustaše and formed the paramilitary arm of the Croatian Party of Rights played a role in the war of independence and their interests were represented in the Croatian parliament, although as the opposition. (The Croatian Party of Rights, HSP, far-right and ultra-nationalism party, gained 7% of votes in the 1992 Croatian parliamentary election and 5% in 1995).

Neo-Ustašism, as Slavko Goldstein called the phenomenon of ultranationalism in Croatia, has a long legacy, and it is still alive and prospering in a variety of forms. Miroslav Škoro's far-right ultranationalist party, the Homeland Movement, won 10.6% and 16 seats in 2020. The presence of the far-right in the political arena finds ways through the Croatian administration to reach museum institutions, whose directors are appointed by the state, although external pressure from the international community exercises a strong influence on Croatia, especially since its entry into the EU. As a result, Tuđman's project of Jasenovac memorial was abandoned after harsh criticism. Currently, Jasenovac hosts the holocaust memorial and museum, built following the design of other holocaust museums in Europe (Milošević and Touquet, 2018; Radonić, 2011).

In 1999 Tuđman died. The following general elections were won by social democrats and marked a critical change in Croatia's history. The HSP scored 5.2% in alliance with the Christian Democratic Union (HKDU). This result was a clear sign of the people's will for change and democracy in Croatia. Three years later, in 2003, the country started accession negotiations to the European Union, which also influenced its trend in terms of heritage memory. The crimes of both fascist and communist regimes were openly recognised, and democracy was advertised as the future of Croatia, a new member of the EU. Museums followed this trend, although the narrative of victimisation didn't disappear. Croatian museums continued to present the nation more as a victim, diminishing or concealing events that could show the violent arm of Croatian nationalism, in particular vis-à-vis the "greater-Serbian aggression" or "homeland war" as Croats call the war fought against the Serbs-led Yugoslav army (1991–1995).

As important as this war was for contemporary Croatia, there isn't much in museums. The same is true for the socialist past of the country, which is mostly absent or underrepresented. The reasons are to be found in Croatian politics, which has had the tendency not to take a clear stance on troublesome historical events (Lukic, 2011). Even national museums, such as the National History Museum in Zagreb, justify the absence of exhibits on the heritage of socialism by mentioning structural problems such as an alleged lack of space. Museums that, like Zagreb's City Museum, have a small exhibit on Croatia's socialist past, emphasise the evils of it. More space is given to the Hapsburg period and post-communism, and the tendency is to obliterate 40 years of history. The same is true for the Ottoman occupation, whose history pertains to an even more distant past, suffering therefore an even deeper suppression. Besides potentially veritable issues such as lack of resources, the main reason for the gap in socialist and Ottoman representations is political, and lies in the attempt of presenting Croatia as a primarily Western European country beyond dichotomies of fascism and communism, that is Christian catholic, certainly not protestant and definitely not Muslim. These dichotomies still divide Croatian politics and the public. As Czerwiński put it, there's claustrophobic state affairs existing in Croatian public debate, whereby the left elites still call the right-wing politicians "fascist" and the rightists depict the left-wing as "communist" and/or "Yugoslavist". The seemingly impossible task of resolving past conflicts is reflected, although subtly and silently, in the silence of Croatian museums dealing with troublesome history.

Paradoxically, contemporary art museums and galleries, such as the Museum of Contemporary Art (MSU) and other minor galleries, exhibit more troubled history than history museums. Unlike Hungary, where the art scene is very much under governmental control, art exhibits in Croatia are more critical of both the present and past. This is true when considering some noteworthy exhibits, such as Sandra Vitaljic's Unfertile Grounds or Reflections of Time 1945–1955, organised by the Klovićevi dvori Gallery in Zagreb. Regarding Vitaljic, her exhibit shows photographs of sites where traumatic events are "in absentia" and traces of past violence are no more visible (Potkonjac and Pletenac, 2016: 75), a clear reference to Croatia's turbulent history and the lost opportunities to come to terms with it. Some, indeed few, exhibits about WW2 and the Holocaust have been held by the Croatian History Museum. I refer to Who's Shootin' Over There? organised by Rhea Ivanuš Petra Braun in 2017 and If I Forget You—The Holocaust in Croatia 1941–1945 / Final Destination Auschwitz, which was one of the few very impressive projects on the Holocaust authored by Nataša Mataušić. However, these are temporary exhibits that last a few months. There is no permanent exhibit, which confirms little engagement by state-sponsored institutions on subjects that could shed a shadow on the nation. This phenomenon was noticed also by Rivera back in 2008: Croatian governments have dealt with the country's past mostly through covering and cultural reframing rather than open acknowledgement (Rivera, 2008).

Interestingly, besides public museums, private ones funded by wealthy and less wealthy individuals go against the tide. Among them, the War Photography Museum and Zagreb 80s Museum, both objects of this study, but also the Red History Museum in Dubrovnik and other private galleries exhibiting on historical issues, including socialism. These museums and exhibits are recent and unstudied phenomena. In particular, the Red History Museum and Zagreb 80s Museum exhibit reconstructions of everyday life in former Yugoslavia through the exhibit of 80s objects, house ambient, and environments. The reasons for building them are many, including (but not limited to) nostalgia, business opportunities, and political activism. Investigating both exhibits and founding motives behind these museums will add further pieces to the complex puzzle of museum politics in Croatia. What seems to be certain is that these private museums fill a void left by the politics of memory, becoming popular destinations for domestic and international tourism.

Case studies

The Image of War Museum is in Zagreb city centre, close to Zrinjevac Park, one of the most beautiful and oldest parks of the city, surrounded by plane trees and kiosks. The museum is not very visible from the street, being in an apartment on the first floor of a building, but since its opening, in July 2018, it enjoys both national and international reputation. It is a private museum, one of those cases where private businesses capitalise on historical events that do not find expression in state museums. As reported by the founder and actual owner of the museum, it fills a gap. Both domestic and especially international tourists want to know about the war that shook Croatia between 1991 and 1995: the "Homeland War" or "Greater Serbian Aggression" as someone calls it (Interview with I.). His words are reflected by the many enthusiastic reviews of the Image of War Museum in websites dedicated to Croatian tourism. And yet, it is not a museum in the strict sense of the word. There are no artefacts to exhibit but a series of photographs that define it best as a gallery, not a museum. The word "museum" was chosen as part of a business strategy, believing that it would give it more visibility, legitimacy, and finally, would render it more profitable (Interview with V., curator of the museum). This marketing strategy is very much in line with other private and even public museums we encounter in this book, such as the Panorama Museum 1453, the Istanbul Museum of Islamic Science and Technology, the 80s museum in Zagreb, or the House of the Hungarian Millennium in Budapest, which do not exhibit any historical artefacts but replicas. It says much about the symbolic power of the word "museum" and its potential to produce revenue.

Business was one reason for building this museum, but it was not the only one. The founder lived through the years of the Homeland War that determined the birth of the Croatian nation-state as we know it in the present. His declared goal, when answering the question "Why have you built this museum?" was: "To make people sick" (Interview with I.). In his mind, to make people sick is to make them see the horrors of the war, the tragedy unfolding in front of their eyes, the dead bodies lying on the street, buildings wrecked, the necessity of peace but also the one of remembering.

The act of remembering becomes here a troublesome one. Who and how to remember? The Homeland War was an ethnic war between people who in the pre-war period lived side by side and mingled within Yugoslavia, a supranational entity. The expression itself "Homeland War" is Croatian. Serbs call it "War in Croatia". This museum is a museum made by Croats in Croatia, and one of the very first problems was the perspective through which the war was to be represented. Could a Croatian perspective do justice to Serbian victims? How to do so? The founder hired a curator, and as often happens, a process of adapting the founder's expectation and the curator's goal began.

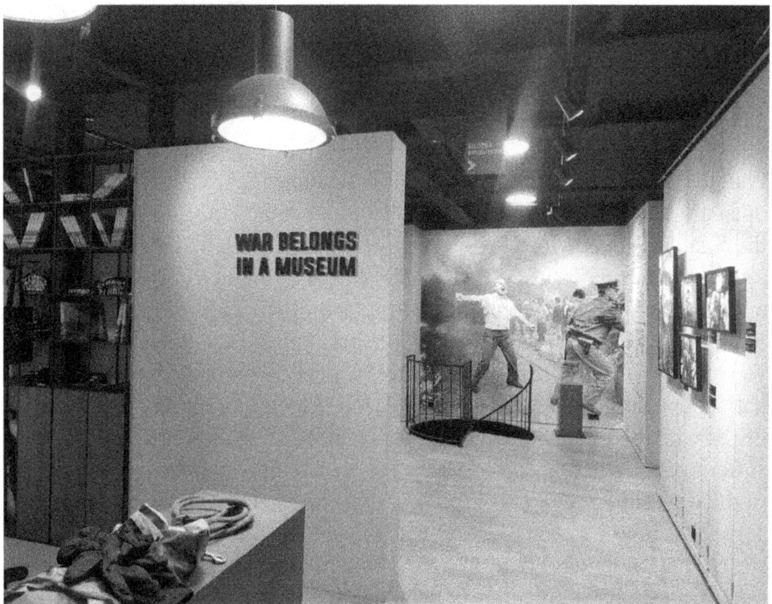

Figure 5.1 War belongs in a museum.

Source: Picture from the exhibit. Credit Image of War Museum.

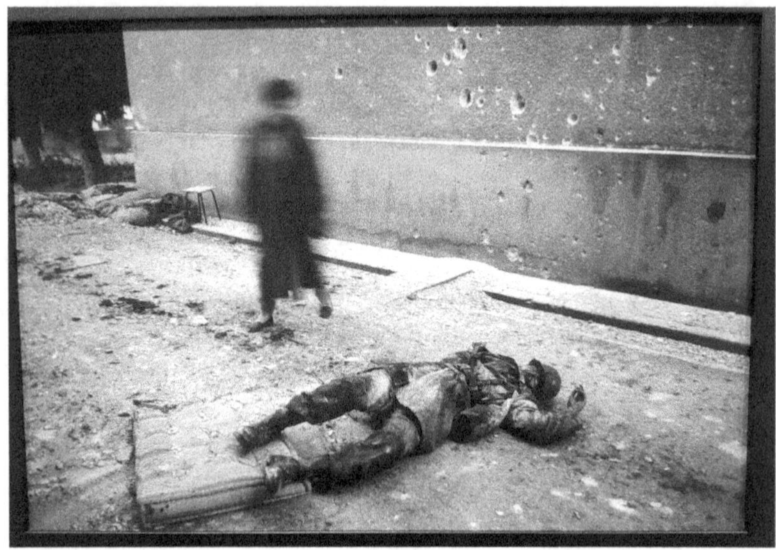

Figure 5.2 'An executed YPA officer the morning after the Croatian forces captured the main barracks. Bjelovar, October 1991'. Original description.

Source: Picture from the exhibit. Credit Image of War Museum. Photographer Christopher Morris.

Founder and curator carried out friendly relationships. V. refers to him as an open mind who didn't interfere with her job. Yet they talked about balancing the founder's needs for playing safe and having a product that doesn't take risks by departing from well-established trends, both in terms of installations and narrative. This might have been one factor that hindered the curator from representing a different and radical 'perspective on the war in Croatia' (Interview with V.). In the curator's mind, this war is still narrated through mainly a national perspective. In her view, in ex-Yugoslavian countries, 'each country deals [with the war] with their own perspective. Croatians only talk about the suffering of Croatians and in Serbia it's always only about their perspective of the war' (Interview with V.). These extracts are interesting insofar as they show the curator's awareness of nationalism and yet her difficulty and inner struggle to go beyond it. She began the curatorial work by inviting photographers from different countries to show their pictures in the museum. This was 'a small attempt to bring different perspectives in' (Interview with V.). Another attempt was through the collection of testimonies, but 'nationalism is still present' she says, and this is a factor that made Serbs 'think they're

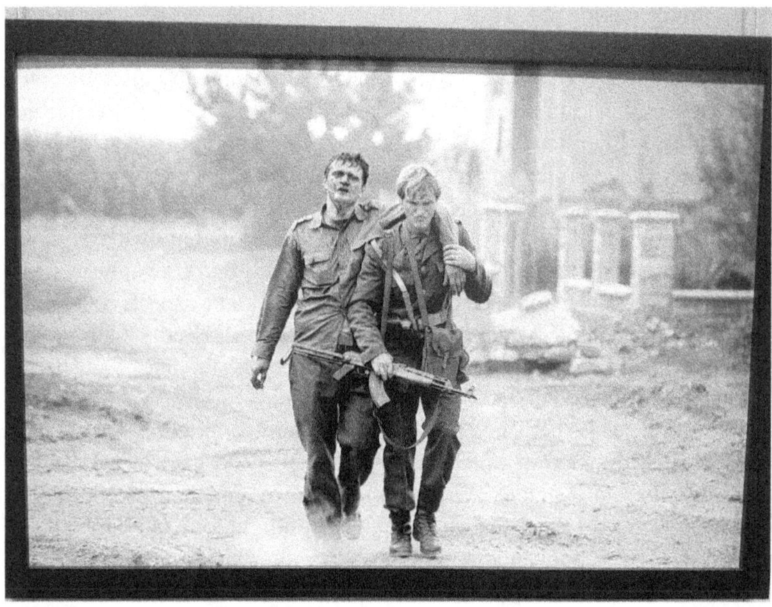

Figure 5.3 'A 19-year-old YPA soldier from the district of Vukovar aids a wounded comerade. Later the same day, he was killed in further action while helping the wounded. Vukova, Borovo Selo, 1991'. Original description.

Source: Picture from the exhibit. Credit Image of War Museum. Photographer Srdjan Sulejmanovic.

not welcome to participate' (Interview with V.). The museum collected testimonies of those who lived through the war but the curator reported that the Serbian community in Croatia didn't take part.

> It's insane because this [nationalism] still influences our life and it's so easy to manipulate people. Whenever you bring this topic people start fighting and they don't deal with any topics that are, you know, our present or future. It's just the past. . . . We still have problematic relationships with Serbia . . . it's all still charged with politics. It's very sensitive how you discuss this topic with somebody from Serbia, even with the open-minded people it's still a painful topic . . . my impression is people in Serbia always felt this guilt imposed on them.

The guilt V. talks about is the one of belonging to the side that started hostilities. However, de facto the museum made minor efforts towards collecting the memories of the Serbian community, which wasn't addressed directly. The curator reports she wasn't involved in the collection of these memories. There was a call by the museum, but they left it to chance. The curator reported that perhaps contacting the Serbian community directly would have helped: 'and they would have come. I know people from the Serbian community' (Interview with V.). There was no committee that included members of the Serbian community who could have taken part in the process of decision-making regarding the choice of the photographs (both in terms of subject and numbers) and about the positioning of these photographs, texts, and so on. This was a shortcoming that probably weighed heavily in the final exhibit. One of the most problematic aspects is the number of photographs showing the suffering of Croats and Serbs. In the whole exhibit, which counts more than a hundred pictures, the ones focusing on Serbs can be counted on the fingers of one hand.

V. reported that she wanted to exhibit a photograph telling the story of the Zec's family, a family of ethnic Serbs, Mihajlo Zec, his wife Marija, and their 12-year-old daughter, Aleksandra, killed by Croatian paramilitaries. The story is one of those that came into the spotlight for its brutality, being the body of Alexandra and her mother found, after investigations started in 1991, in a garbage dump. 12-year-old Alexandra had her hands tied, a tie covering her eyes, several shots into her head, wounds on her right cheek and three more over her right ear. The curator reported she didn't find a picture that could tell the story.

> the only image that I knew of was an image of this location when it burned down, but unfortunately the photographer who shot this image is a really nationalistic one, so when I asked him if I can have this image for the exhibition, of course, he said no. It was easy to understand why I wanted this image. Then I thought, should I put there like a blind spot like one empty frame there? But I was not sure, and because I thought, maybe then I will make the whole exhibition about this empty frame, which was also not right. I'm just trying to paint for you how difficult it was actually to decide. That's why I think I was not radical enough with my representation of the war.
>
> (Interview with V.)

Nationalism seems to play a role here as an element favoring deception, in particular by concealing the material proof of a past that could benefit Serbs, perceived here as antagonists. More interestingly, the curator opens to self-criticism and refers to the fact that she wasn't 'radical enough' with her representation of the war. In her eyes, to be radical would be to show the suffering of both Serbs and Croats equally, using the same standards and beyond nationalist lens. That the curator couldn't achieve this result is not to attribute to her failure and her failure only. We must consider here the ideological and organisational strength and the pervasiveness of nationalism as elements hindering a better response. In fact, what these extracts show is the power of nationalism. Even in a free setting where professionals were free to express and exhibit critical thinking, the curator couldn't design the museum she envisaged. Finally, it strikes that, in the world of nation-states and nationalism, designing a radical exhibition on the Homeland War is to show that the suffering of Serbs and Croats is, to the very core, the suffering of fellow human beings. Beyond flags and anthems, in the very act of suffering and dying, this is what they were: human beings. Nationalism hinders the show of this very evidence, burying it under words such as "us" and "them".

For the sake of clarity, the curator confirmed that Serbs who visited the museum also reported that it doesn't exhibit enough on Serbian suffering. Vis-à-vis this criticism, the curator's doubts about her own work increased. And yet, she attempted to explain the logic behind her choices. It is in this fragment that she reported about the "nuances" that she introduced, which is her way not to pave the way to nationalist interpretations of the exhibit. The curator highlights that during the war, Croatian propaganda newspapers would publish mostly heroic photographs of Croats, and Serbian soldiers were portrayed as "beasts" (Interview with V.). She said: 'in this exhibit you have the image of a Serbian soldier carrying a wounded one and that's quite an heroic image [Figure 5.3]. You're not supposed to see a heroic Serbian soldier in an exhibition on the Croatian war. It's a strong statement' (Interview with V.). The fact that one is not supposed to see a heroic Serbian soldier in an exhibition on the Croatian war tells much about how the spectrum of exhibits about the Homeland War tends towards one-sided nationalist representations. The presence of Figure 5.2, which shows a YPA soldier executed and left on the street, attempts to break with these representations, suggesting that Croats recurred to the same methods as Serbs. In addition, it is a way for the curator to show that the horrors of the war affected both parts. There are photographs of Serbian civilians that the curator chose to show the fear and uncertainty in the eyes of the Serbian community, among which are photographs of children, the quintessential innocent. When clarifying her curatorial choices, V. is keen to stress the difference between the Image of War Museum and other exhibitions by official institutions that 'are having greater impact [than the Image of War Museum] on the public opinion and how the war is officially remembered' (Interview with V.). She refers to Faces of War, Dubrovnik during the Homeland War, all held by the Croatian History Museum. Those exhibitions, V. reports 'reflect to a greater extent the national paradigm and discourse on memorialisation of the war' (Interview with A.). When browsing the dedicated websites to these exhibits—they were temporary, therefore the only way to investigate them is through catalogues and websites—the difference V. talks about strikes clear. There is no trace of Serbian suffering. The reason is given by the Croatian History Museum and it is enlightening of the way nationalism worms into state museums and influences them:

> The photographs on display are exclusively the works of Croatian photographers. . . . Photographs from the occupied parts of Croatia, as well as photographs of certain key events during the Homeland War (such as the tragic fall of Vukovar) are similarly not on display in this exhibition because they could only have been taken by foreign and Serbian war photographers. The reliability and objectivity of published photographs, particularly those released during the war, can always be questioned given their manipulative and media/propagandistic role.
>
> (Extract from Faces of War—Croatian History Museum, July 9th 2015–September 20th, 2015)[1]

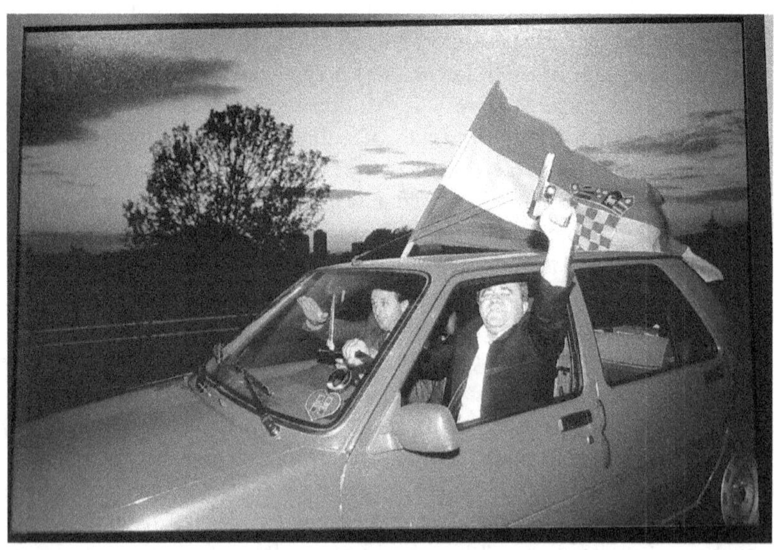

Figure 5.4 'Citizens of Zagreb celebrate the referendum results, which proclaimed Croatia's independence and its separation from Yugoslavia. May 19, 1991'. Original description from the exhibit.

Source: Picture from the exhibit. Credit Image of War Museum. Photographer Paul Lowe.

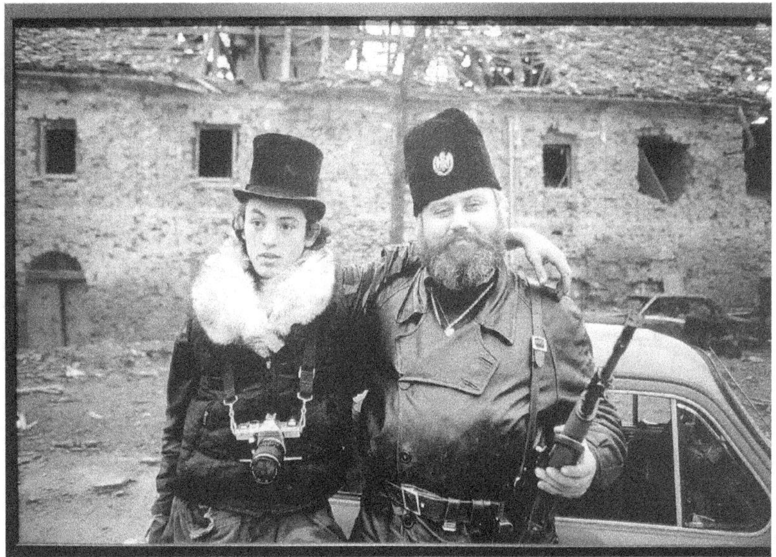

Figure 5.5 'Serbian father and son pose in the newly captured territory. Vukovar, 1991'. Original description from the exhibit.

Source: Picture from the exhibit. Credit Image of War Museum. Photographer Ron Haviv.

Among the nuances that the curator exhibited in the museum, there are two photographs that when placed side by side (they aren't side by side in the exhibition) assume a meaningful message in both societies in the present. It's the specter of ultra-nationalism, suggested by the fascist salute, the national flag, and the pistol that the driver holds in Figure 5.4, and the Chetnik uniform of the father in Figure 5.5. There is a sense of drama in both photographs. They were shot to celebrate, but within the context of the exhibit there is nothing glorious in those celebrations. The wrecked building behind the father and son in Figure 5.5 hints at the uselessness of war. What it leaves behind, the curator seems to hint here, is death and ruins. When considering that in recent years both countries have been crossed by extreme nationalist movements that reached power positions, these pictures represent a timely warning that such tragic events could happen again. This is the merit of the Image of War Museum, which does what state museums couldn't. The fascist salute here is an explicit reference to the Ustaše, whose heritage didn't disappear in around 40 years of communism, resurfaced strongly during the Homeland War, and entered the Croatian political arena soon after (Pavlaković, 2008). Croatian nationalism in all its forms, including neo-Ustašism, affected the post-war era in the 1990s and keeps affecting in the 2020s the way Croats represent the Homeland War, the Jewish Holocaust, Serbian genocide, the communist era, and other historical events in the Croatian past. This is what the case study of the Image of War Museum seems to suggest. Finally, although this museum has the indisputable merit of dealing with the Homeland War in a whole different way from state museums, its original premise remains unfulfilled. The museum was curated by extremely educated professionals in their field, who aimed to exhibit the war outside nationalist lenses, and even in this setting nationalism wasn't openly questioned.

This is even more clear when analysing the way Croatian museums exhibit about the Holocaust and Serbian genocide. Regarding this subject, I focused on the Jasenovac Memorial Site Museum, where I carried out several interviews with the personnel, in particular with people in charge of the exhibit, the museum director, and historians who reviewed the museum when it was redesigned in 2004 (an earlier version of the museum had been established in 1968) and reopened in 2006. The first important evidence is that Jasenovac is far from any urban center. It takes over an hour from the capital Zagreb to reach it. No other permanent exhibit exists in other Croatian cities. This is the only national museum exhibiting on WW2 in Croatia (Interview with I.), which says much about the will of Croatian governments to deal with a potentially troublesome past. There is a kind of quiet around WW2 and related events that is explainable through the fact that breaking it could give birth to trouble, in particular because WW2 events are linked not only to the Holocaust but also to the genocide of Serbs, which is inextricably linked to sensitive subjects in the present such as the Homeland War.

The current exhibit hasn't been renovated in 15 years. Some plastic covers of information panels are so damaged that it's impossible to read through them. The general feeling, confirmed by interviews with the museum personnel, is that this museum was needed to comply with EU requests when Croatia started accession negotiations. After that, not much funding was provided for regular maintenance, let alone renovation or new museum complexes dealing with this subject. The economic element is fundamental to explain how Croatian governments avoid exhibiting on WW2 events. It is a way to escape potential criticism that inevitably targets those who attempt to deal with this past in Croatia.

In fact, as small as it is—the main exhibit is 250 square meters—this place was at the center of harsh criticism that explains the lack of similar exhibits. Criticism included the fact that this Jasenovac Memorial Site Museum 1) follows a model of memorialisation of the Holocaust that is led by USA and Yad Vashem; 2) doesn't provide much information about

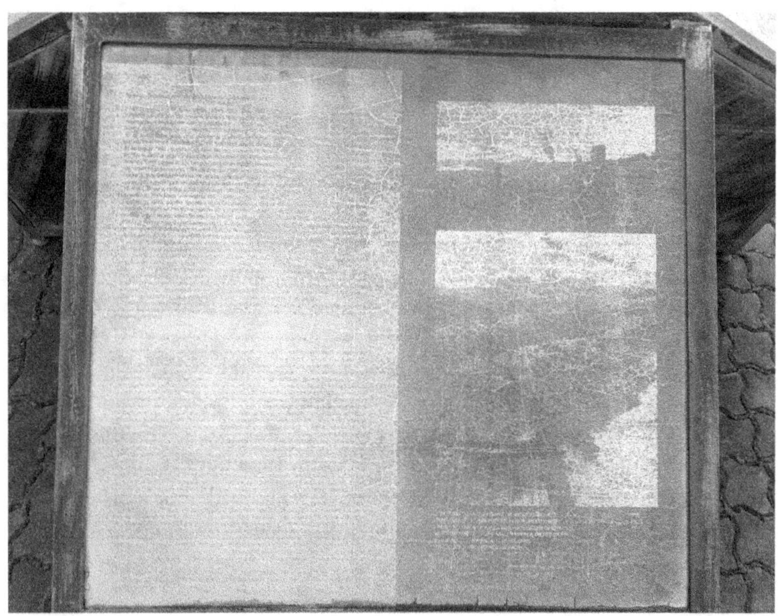

Figure 5.6 Information panel worn out by time.

the ideology of Nazism, fascism, and their Croatian equivalent; 3) doesn't provide much information about the concentration camp itself but focuses on individual stories of suffering; 4) doesn't provide enough information on Roma people, and when it does, it makes use of stereotypes; and 5) doesn't provide enough information about the perpetrators, in particular it doesn't place enough emphasis on the Ustaše as perpetrators.

Interviews with curators and reviewers of the museum have shown their openness to ward off this criticism and accept the fact that 'many things could have been done differently' (Interview with N.). However, they stressed that at the basis of these mistakes there was no attempt at revisionism. When I told them that some critics such as Julija Koš went as far as saying that the memorial seemed designed by the Ustaše and that 'such a museum in Jasenovac should be closed' (Van der Laarse, 2013: 82), one reviewer of the museum said:

> I can't comment on this because she's exaggerating. One can say that we don't have the biography of the most notorious criminals of Jasenovac, there is no picture of them or descriptions, well, you can say that

> with additional space you would be able to present them but given the space at disposal, it was impossible to cover all subjects. . . . But the way pro-Ustaše circles describe the exhibition is completely different from the exhibition itself. You cannot say that.
>
> (Interview with J.)

Julija Koš's criticism might be politically based in the sense that she sees any sign of weakness—in this specific case, a sign of weakness might be the fact that the museum doesn't show any photograph of mass killings or any other material that might shock the visitor—as potentially exploitable by neo-Ustaše's attempts to historical revisionism. We're confronted here with the question of how to present a painful national heritage in a highly polarised society that experiences the resurgence of nationalism also in its extreme forms. Divisions exist between those who support stronger proofs that elicit deeper emotional responses and those who support more symbolism, individualisation of victims, and less emphasis on the horrific methods of killing, such as the Ustaše knife, which was no longer exhibited after 2006 (Van der Laarse, 2013). The latter is not inevitably the choice of revisionism, although it might be exploited for that, but a choice through reflection led by the goal of remembering the past in a way that doesn't fuel hatred and revanchism.

The political exploitation of these different views gave birth to a heated debate that favours the stalemate in present Croatia's representations of the war. Politicians are not willing to put themselves in the position to be potentially criticised by all segments of Croatian politics, and beyond. Representing memories of such a sensitive subject has repercussions also on the international stage, especially as it increases the already high tension between Croatia and Serbia around these events. Jasenovac has been and continues to be a motive for tension that revolves around several elements, including the way the genocide is exhibited in Croatia and above all the official number of victims. This number varies according to political affiliation, which once again explains why museums are targets of politicians with a nationalist agenda: They collect and exhibit historical evidence. The Jasenovac Memorial Site and Museum played an important role in this sense, researching the names and numbers of those who died in the concentration camp. As Kolstø (2011) and Benčić (2018) stated, the range goes from gross exaggeration (over 1 million victims) to complete minimisation (30,000) and denial. Serbian authorities have recently referred to 700,000 and Croatian authorities to 81,998 victims (Chrzová, 2018). According to J., 'if 700,000 people were killed in Jasenovac in 1945, then everything that happened in 1991–1995, the siege of Sarajevo, the atrocities and mass crimes in Srebrenica, and so and so forth [committed by the Bosnian Serb Army of Republika Srpska (VRS)] against Muslims but also against Croats, were some kind of revenge' (Interview with J.). In the minds of many, such an act would be justifiable in view of what happened in the past.

In the present, many studies—including some carried out by Serbian academics—bring evidence that the number of victims in Jasenovac varies from 100,000 to 200,000 and it is difficult to determine it more precisely because of the destruction of relevant documents. Yet, nationalism-led governments continue to use data that support their ideological positions and overlook the others. In Croatia, this produces fear of exacerbating tension and results in the fact that 'everything is very slow . . .', as reported by one member of the directive in Jasenovac suggesting that the stalemate in representations of the war is because of the current political scenario (Interview with I.).

Indeed, for J., the present political scenario is worse than 15 years ago (Interview with J.). The politics of memory has been recently influenced by ultranationalist elements within the ruling coalition party, the HDZ. Ultranationalist forces attempt to win management positions within museums, exhibit revisionist versions of sensitive historical events, and influence the population. Also Jasenovac was targeted by ultranationalists when a controversial plaque with the Ustaša's slogan *Za dom spremni* ('For homeland—ready!') appeared nearby the memorial site in 2016. The plaque remained there for 10 months before being removed—after numerous protests—and placed in the nearby town of Novska. Interestingly, the plaque was installed by former members of the Croatian Defence Forces (HOS), neo-Ustaše who fought in the Homeland War and right-wing politicians whose goal was to commemorate 11 fighters who died during the 1991–1995 war. It was an attempt to symbolically take possession of Jasenovac that can be explained only through the fact that the legacy of Ustašism is still alive and perceived as a legitimate political goal in Croatia. Museums and other cultural institutions are targeted as places where this legitimisation occurs and spreads to a wider popular scale.

The situation was different 'when the Jasenovac Memorial Site Museum was designed' (2004–2006) (Interview with J.). Ivo Sanader was Prime Minister back then:

> He pushed a European view on the Holocaust and genocide and it doesn't matter that he was conservative, a moderate right government. He was fully aware of the fact that Croatia's strong revisionism supported by part of the Croatian nationalists wasn't going to be accepted by the EU. So, he was controlling this rightist conservatism, this revisionism, and all these things that for Europe are pro-fascism or pro-Nazi . . . and he succeeded.
>
> (Interview with J.)

For J., Sanader left curators in Jasenovac free to do their work. The exhibition went through a process of review where half of the historians belonged to the Serbian and Jewish community. This would be the proof that there was no attempt at revisionism and that current criticism results from the extreme polarisation in Croatia and politicisation of historical events. Those who, in Croatia, support the idea that the exhibit should elicit greater emotional response not to give way to political manipulation see the Jasenovac Memorial Site Museum as a product of neo-Ustašism. The same is true for nationalist Serbs in Serbia and Croatia, who would like more explicit references to the Croatian perpetrators. Criticism comes also from negationists who reject the whole narrative of the Holocaust and genocide. One of the elements of the exhibit that has been heavily criticised is the focus on the victims, which would come at the cost of a wider perspective of the tragedy of the Holocaust. According to M., another reviewer of the museum, the then museum director Nataša Jovičić involved Yad Vashem in the making of the Jasenovac Memorial Center and that's where the focus on the victims comes from (Interview with M.). It was a shared decision between those in charge of making the museum and Yad Vashem. Reviewers supported the project and the museum came into being. This evidence absolves the Jasenovac Memorial Site Museum from criticism that sees it as a pro-Ustaše institution. At the same time it points to an already known phenomenon, which is the symbolic power of Yad Vashem over representations of the Holocaust. As Radonić (2018) put it, Yad Vashem—Israel's official memorial to the victims of the Holocaust—is an international point of reference for Holocaust museums that leads to standardisation. Also David (2020) pointed to the same phenomenon through a wider research on memorialisation and collective remembrance, highlighting that standardisation based on human rights has 'quite disturbing results' (David, 2020: 9). Rather than producing solidarity, it is 'harvested back by the nation-state to promote nationalist, ethnically based agendas' (David, 2020: 9). The previously mentioned event about the plaque reciting the Ustaša's slogan *Za dom spremni* must be seen through this lens. The same is true for other contexts such as Hungary, where nationalist forces are given free rein and have sponsored a number of museums that promote their nationalist agendas. Unsurprisingly, standardisation also faces other challenges, especially in realities where the high level of particularism doesn't lend itself well to standardisation. Such is the reality of Jasenovac, whose history of the Holocaust is entangled with the Serbian genocide. Here the number of Serbian victims far exceeds the one of Jews.

Perhaps such a different camp, where the Jewish Holocaust and Serbian genocide are inextricably entangled, would need a novel approach, one that the extreme polarisation around these issues and attempt at political exploitation makes it difficult even to think of. What is left is a kind of immobility best expressed through the words of Jasenovac Memorial Site Museum director Ivo Pejakovic: 'I don't have any better solution for that. It's about patience and slowly slowly pushing forward' (Interview with Ivo Pejakovic). Again, the comparison with Hungary might help to show things from a different perspective.

Hungary's memory politics is in a position that is diametrically opposed to the Croatian. Given the number of museums that, built in recent years, address the memory of WW2, Holocaust, and communism era, it is fair to state that the museum landscape in Hungary is more dynamic than in Croatia. One is brought to see the reason for this dynamism in the stability that Fidesz's solid majority granted to Hungary, which sped up decision-making. However, a closer look to the political forces ruling these two countries suggests that the reason might also lie in their different political ideologies. The form that nationalism took in Hungary is a more aggressive form with elements of populism. Fidesz surfed the general malcontent rooted in the financial crisis of 2008 and redirected it towards domestic and foreign elites and immigrants in the decade 2010–2020. Fidesz's nationalism advocates the return to the good old days by reconstituting a more ethnically homogeneous Hungary and returning to traditional national values, whatever this might mean. That's where museums come into essence, as a way of feeding people with nostalgia for a glorious past and restating the centrality of the nation especially vis-à-vis the loss of references brought by the global village (Poll, 2012). This is true in Hungary as in Turkey, two countries sharing also the feature that none of them is considered a free country anymore.[2] Instead, Croatia presents a different situation. Plenkovic's party HDZ is a center-right party and although his coalition includes far-right elements, they are kept at the margin. Most importantly, Croatia doesn't share Hungary's and Turkey's tradition of long decennial governments (Erdoğan is to power for almost 20 years now) and it is still considered a free country. The far right in Croatia was more powerful with Tomislav Karamarko from 2012 to 2016, which is a short window of 4 years that doesn't allow structural changes such as the ones that occurred in Turkey and Hungary. That said, the immobility in Croatia's representations of the Holocaust and Serbian genocide might be seen also as the result of political forces whose agenda doesn't involve aggressive politics of identity such as Hungary's and Turkey's. Indeed, avoiding to give visibility to historical events that are emotionally and politically charged might have been a deliberate choice by Croatian governments to silence a troublesome past and focus more on re-branding Croatia as a Democratic European country. This would be almost like sweeping the past under the rug rather than pouring fuel on the fire.

As well as failing to address the Holocaust and genocide, the communist past finds almost no space in public museums. The City Museum of Zagreb is interesting proof of that, focusing largely on a distant past and containing almost nothing on the recent one. There is only one room dedicated to the second half of the 20th century, which is shared by events related to WW2 and Yugoslavia, although communism in Croatia occupied a large share of the 20th century and its heritage is still alive and vivid in the memories of Croats.

The lack of communist heritage representations in public museums is a gap that Croatian governments haven't and do not seem willing to fill. As it happened for the Homeland War, private businesses took advantage of the situation and filled the void with a private museum: the 80s Museum. This museum is located in the city centre, at walking distance from the larger Croatian History Museum. It occupies the first floor of an old building in the historical part of the city. The official website recites that 'it is dedicated to the present past in a new way. Its space is a reconstruction of everyday life in former Yugoslavia in a unique and interactive way that intersects past & future, way of life & heritage, memories & emotions'.[3] The exhibition is formed by 80s furniture, electronic devices, newspapers, books, gadgets, and all those objects that one could find in an 'average apartment in former Yugoslavia', says the personnel of the museum (Interview with A). The collection was bought from collectors, but it came also as donations (Interview with A.). The visit is advertised highlighting the fact that it's the 'first interactive museum' in Croatia (Interview with A.). Visitors can interact with all exhibited objects without restrictions.

One element that is striking is that object descriptions betray a certain nostalgia for the Yugoslavian past. This is evident in sentences such as 'the majority of housewives were making tapestries, today *it is only a dream*'[4] followed by 'there were lessons how to make tapestries as part of the household education in the elementary school'. The word "dream" betrays here a positive feeling of the curator vis-à-vis the fact that in former Yugoslavia housewives made tapestries. Even more enlightening is the reference to education in former Yugoslavia. Not only tapestries made by housewives are seen as a positive outcome of that society, but the fact that the Yugoslavian state educated those women to do it praises Yugoslavia and communism as the political scenario that made it possible. Similar descriptions abound in the museum.

The exhibition of the 80s Museum depicts a bright and positive past in former Yugoslavia. It does it through the object descriptions although some don't necessarily need them. One of these is erotic magazines. The museum exhibits a number of them in the living room. The visibility given to these objects, which in present culture are relegated to the private sphere, is to suggest that ex-Yugoslavia was more liberal in terms of sexual mores than present Croatia. These objects hint at the idea launched by the much debated 2006 German documentary by André Meier *Do Communists Have Better Sex?* according to which sex was more liberal in communist Germany. While the literature shows no consensus on this subject, what's important here is that these objects are used to provide a positive image of Yugoslavia—less traditional, more progressive, less backward, and more modern than stereotypical images suggest. Other objects such as computers, typewriters, portable radios, and tape players play the same role. By exhibiting these objects the museum suggests that former Yugoslavia was an open society to foreigners and foreign trends. Posters of iconic movies in the 80s such as *Terminator* or *Back to the Future*, which were banned in the Soviet Union and other communist states, or references to international meetings such as the 1987 Universiade, are intended to suggest just this.

An employee of the museum reported that the main reason for building this museum was profit. The inspiration came the Museum of the GDR in Berlin, which A. visited around 10 years ago:

> somehow spontaneously the idea came about when I was searching for some new business since I was fed up with the last one. I felt like I could try with a museum. We had Yugoslavia here. And then we did the market research for it, which showed that's better not to use the word Yugoslavia. That's how we decided to go with "Zagreb 80s".
>
> (Interview with A.)

A. reports that, for her, the 1980s were 'the golden years, without conflicts, wars, new musical genres, the craziest fashion to date, and a great feeling of unity among peoples of the world' (Interview with A.). A museum of the 80s represented a business opportunity, and for business it was made more interactive than others. This museum is a 'live museum . . . with parties and dancing in the weekend' (Interview with A.). In pre-pandemic times it was very successful, especially during the tourism season. Reporters and bloggers came to visit, interviewed A., and advertised the museum worldwide. A. reports that Croats come here out of nostalgia while foreigners come because 'they can have fun here, dress and undress, listen to old records. . . . It's a very relaxed atmosphere for one lovely decade, because the 80s can't be missed. . . . They resurfaced now and became a trend again even in the world of fashion' (Interview with A.).

There were no professional curators for this museum. The founder subleased apartments before opening it: 'we are primarily going for fun, entirely on interaction, so that visitors can wear 80s clothes, have some coffee from

Yugoslavia in *džezva* (cezve), they can smell the perfumes, listen to records, cassettes, sit down into *Fićeka* (the car), go through the books from the period . . . we are really going for one time capsule, throughout all four human senses' (Interview with A.). From this perspective, Hooper-Greenhill was right when, almost 30 years ago, she wrote that 'Today, almost anything may turn out to be a museum. The experience of going to a museum is often closer to that of going to a theme park or a funfair than that which used to be offered by the austere, glass-case museum' (Hooper-Greenhill, 1992: 1). My interviews with the staff of the museum reflects this point. They made it like a theme park to make profit out of it. However, Hooper-Greenhill also wrote that 'Museums are no longer built in the image of that nationalistic temple of culture, the British Museum' (Hooper-Greehill, 1992: 1), and this is only partially true. Most museums do not look like nationalist temples anymore, some may not be built to absolve nationalist purposes, but they still function as nationalist devices, in one way or another. This is true also for the 80s Museum, which was born for business and business only.

The 80s Museum is the second museum of this kind built in Croatia, the first one left already Zagreb for Shanghai, bought by the Chinese government. This detail caught my attention. It doesn't happen often that a museum built in one state is bought entirely by another state and transferred there. When deepening the story of the first 80s Museum, I came to know that the sale happened in 2019, which 'was the Croatian-Chinese year of tourism and friendship' (Interview with A.). A massive Chinese delegation came to Croatia to invest. The ceremony was opened by Premier Li Keqiang and Prime Minister Andrej Plenković at Klovićevi Dvori Gallery.[5] A. reported that 'a young woman from the delegation who is usually involved in museums bought out the license for the exhibit from us, for 10 years. And each year she will have it in a different city in China. To show around Zagreb in the 80s' (Interview with A.). It is not difficult to imagine why the Chinese were interested in Zagreb 80s Museum. While A. used the words "to show Zagreb in the 80s" what she meant was "to show communist Zagreb to communist China". It's an exercise of national narcissism. The fun atmosphere which A. curated for business purposes gave the museum a relaxed atmosphere and celebratory setting that struck a chord with the Chinese delegation. They saw in it a way to advertise a positive example of communism outside China, which is another face of nationalist propaganda in which the Chinese government is increasingly investing (Liu and Zhou, 2019). The Balkans serve this purpose well. It's a region that was under communist influence for decades. The possibility to show the positive side of this influence and overlook the negative one is an opportunity that Chinese politicians grasped without hesitation. Also for Croatia, the museum was an opportunity. Although it is a private museum, the Croatian government didn't hesitate to use it to strengthen its relationships with China.[6]

The communist past of Croatia is used here as a springboard for political and economic profit, with China being a powerful investor, and therefore, an ally. This is made clear by Croatian Ambassador Dario Mihelin at the opening of the museum in Shanghai, who reported, 'Croatian-Chinese and China relations are moving forward, bringing us closer together, not only politically and economically, but in the general social and cultural sense' (*Croatia News*, 2019). This discourse is justified by the number of Chinese tourists visiting Croatia, which increased meteorically in recent years and reached half a million tourists by the end of 2019. In this perspective, it is not surprising that Croatia is interested in strengthening its relations with China and use museum institutions to attract Chinese interest, if needed.

Finally, the case studies investigated in this chapter brought further evidence of and detailed the role played by nationalism in Croatian museums. None of these museums are "national museums" in the traditional sense of this word and yet nationalism played a major role in their making and their exhibits. After reaching similar results in the investigation of museums in Turkey and Hungary, this chapter reinforces the idea that the presence of nationalism in museums is structural and goes beyond the museum typology. All museums are subject to nationalism in one way or another.

Unlike the previous chapter on Turkey, this chapter was enriched by data on a museum that attempted to resist nationalism. The Image of War Museum is one of the two case studies of museums (the other one is the HDKE, Chapter 3) contributing to substantiate the idea that nationalism is not all-powerful and can be, and sometimes is, challenged. And yet, although the qualitative nature of this book doesn't lend itself to statistical analysis, the fact that only two from more than ten museums investigated in this book share this characteristic reinforces the idea that nationalism dominates the museum.

This chapter was also the second chapter, after Hungary's, which investigated a Holocaust museum. The events around the Jasenovac Memorial Site Museum confirm the power of nationalism attempting to take over places that put supranational values, such as human rights, above national ones. Events such as the Holocaust have the power of silencing nationalism, they overshadow it, or worse, dismantle the positive aura that nationalists create around the nation and reveal nationalism's darkest sides. In this perspective, it is unsurprising that both nationalist forces in Hungary and Croatia wormed or attempted to worm their way through the Holocaust museums in their countries, promoting softer versions of their nations' involvement in the Holocaust. This data represents further evidence supporting the thesis that nationalism doesn't like to be questioned. One of the features of nationalism is national priority, which in the case of the museum means staging positive representations of the nation, even at times at the cost of historical evidence.

Notes

1 Faces of War—Croatian History Museum, at www.hismus.hr/en/exhibitions/past-exhibitions/faces-war/# (Last accessed 08/03/2021)
2 Freedom House has declassed Turkey to the status "Not free" while Hungary was declassed to "Partly free". Croatia is considered a "free country". Countries and Territories | Freedom House (Last accessed 10/04/2021)
3 At www.zagreb80.com/ (Last accessed 04/03/2021)
4 Description of tapestries exhibited by the museum. My emphasis.
5 For pictures please visit http://vn.china-embassy.org/eng/xwdt/t1653776.htm (Last accessed 04/21/2021)
6 For pictures of the Croatian Ambassador Dario Mihelin and the Chinese delegation in Shanghai at the opening of the museum: www.croatiaweek.com/zagreb-in-the-80s-museum-opens-in-shanghai/ (Last accessed 04/21/2021)

6 Final thoughts

On October 24, 1995, the University of Warwick hosted a debate, known today as the "Warwick Debate", where Ernest Gellner, one of the most prominent scholars of nationalism, and his former student Anthony Smith, discussed the origins of nationalism. Gellner and Smith articulated their ideas and laid the foundation for two different and yet equivalently popular theories of nationalism: Anthony Smith's ethno-symbolism and Ernest Gellner's modernist theory. In brief, the first projected nations back to thousands of years, while the second defended his thesis that nations are modern constructions.[1] The pivotal moment of the debate was when Gellner asked Smith: "Do nations have navels?". Explaining his question, Gellner said, 'you may fall about laughing, but obviously if Adam was created by God at a certain date, let's say 4,003 bc, obviously I mean it's a prima facie first reaction that he didn't have a navel, so to say, because Adam did not go through the process by which people acquire navels' (Smith, 1996: 373). The core of Gellner's question was that, if nations have navels—the material evidence of cycles of national reproductions dating thousands of years—, they should be visible and we should be able to see them. Hence "Do nations have navels?" The debate didn't have a winner, and scholars are still divided between creationists and anti-creationists, with some believing that nations have navels, while others don't.

What does this debate have to do with the museum? As I have attempted to prove in this book, museums have navels, national navels. Not only the birth of the museum is inextricably linked to the birth of nationalism and its changes through history, but in the present, all museums, regardless of the subject they cover or their status as private or public museum, are born in a world where nationalism is the dominant political ideology. National identity is one of the primary sources of self-identification, and the nation-state is the dominant political territorial reality. As such, they are tied to the nation-state system and its ideology through an umbilical cord that feeds them national symbols, national taxonomies, national histories, myths, and

DOI: 10.4324/9781003053033-7

so on. These elements are visible and mark the museum as a national entity. Even when the umbilical cord is severed and the museum turns to subjects that apparently have nothing to do with nationalism, say, art or science, or museums that are strongly oriented towards profit, navels remain in the form of national flags, taxonomies, insignias, and other symbols. In this perspective, the evidence collected in this book suggests that the impact of nationalism on the museum is enormous, much stronger than previous studies have acknowledged, and goes beyond the construction of national museums as political tools of the elites that contribute to national identity.

The relationship between nationalism and the museum is marked by the domination of the first over the latter. Expressing a similar form of domination in society, Pierre Bourdieu said, 'we are born determined and we have a small chance of ending up free' (Bourdieu and Chartier, 2015: 20), meaning that 'being born in a social world, we accept a whole range of postulates, axioms which go without saying and require no inculcating' (Bourdieu and Wacquant, 1992: 168). The same is true for the museum. National postulates and axioms that go without saying are the norm in museums, and although breaking up with and gaining liberation from nationalism is not impossible, it's rare and implies a struggle on the part of the agents within it. Paraphrasing and adapting Gellner's famous simile to the world of the museum, a nation has its museums as a man has a nose and two ears, 'a deficiency in any of these particulars is not inconceivable . . . but only as result of some disaster, and it is itself a disaster of a kind' (Gellner, 1983: 6). No Croatian flag flies on the British museum, and the reason is that the British museum is British like the Louvre is French. But there exists an historical photograph of the Petit Palais in Paris (art museum within the complex of museums around the Louvre) flying the Nazi flag after the Nazis occupied the city. The event was, to use Gellner's expression, the result of a disaster for the French, but also the symbol of German nationalism's victory. This says much about the power of nationalism in museums and the extent to which national symbols give body to them. More than mere decorations, they determine power, belonging, and identity.

Acknowledging that nationalism is a structural presence in society, and as a consequence, also in museums, is to question the deeply embedded assumption that political ideologies, worming their way through the museum, originate from and are the reflection of the elites. This study suggests that a more holistic view of the museum is needed as the intersection of groups that participate in the reproduction of nationalism. In most of the case studies investigated, museums were commissioned by elites who espoused nationalism, but they were not the only ones involved in their making. Indeed, if one excludes the commissioners, elites weren't involved much. Museums were designed and built by architects, archaeologists,

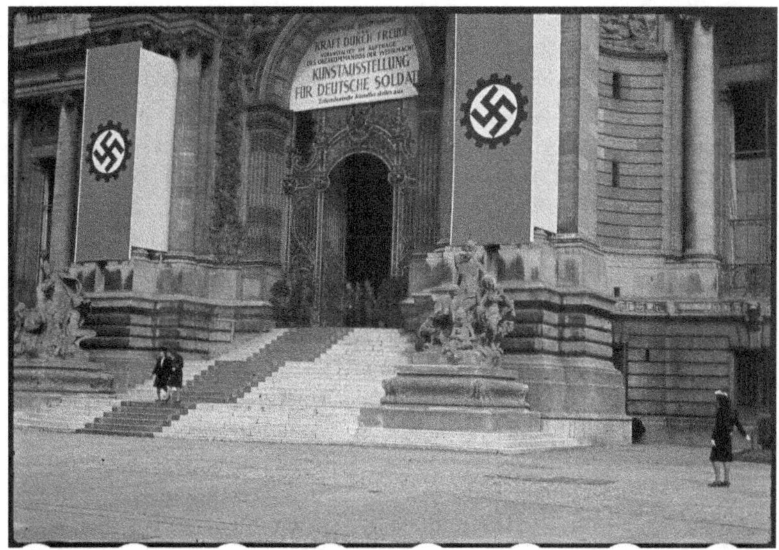

Figure 6.1 Petit Palais under Nazi occupation.

Source: Photograph by André Zucca.

historians, and other experts. These were no elites, especially if one considers elites as those who occupy positions 'from which they can look down upon, so to speak, and by their decisions mightily affect, the everyday worlds of ordinary men and women' (Mills, 2000 [1956]: 1). In addition, after their building, museums were managed by bureaucrats, for example, museum directors, secretaries, and others who were also not elite, and yet played an important role in the museum. All of them shared or complied with nationalism at a twofold level. The first is the structural level, which implies accepting the natural existence of the nation, the second is the superstructural level, which involves all that is superficial and yet fundamental to give body to the nation, the fact that it has certain imagined characteristics, a certain past, traditions, and so on.

In the case of Turkey (Chapter 4), Erdoğan's Justice and Development Party (AKP) commissioned the construction of the Istanbul Museum of the History of Science and Technology in Islam but historians and architects who shared the party ideology materially made the museum, giving body to the idea of science and technology as national matters. After the construction work was completed, bureaucrats kept the museum working and exhibiting, often with the same verve as the designer of the museum, advertising the museum as a Turkish museum, showing it to the people at large, contacting schools, organising school trips, and so on. The influence of groups other than power elites is even more clear in the Panorama Museum 1453 (still Chapter 4), a museum whose political elites didn't visit until its opening and whose concept and exhibit was entirely produced by a group of artists. The Image of War Museum (Chapter 5), a private museum in Zagreb, showed similar dynamics as did other museums in Hungary and Croatia. That said, without being grounded in a variety of groups and social forces, in structure and subjectivities, nationalism couldn't be so pervasive and present in the museum.

This is not to say that politicians with a nationalist agenda do not enormously affect the museum and therefore do not merit special attention. They do. In many cases this agenda was at the origin of the museum, the substitution of a museum director, the "restructuring" of an exhibit, and so on. Indeed, evidence gathered in this study supports the hypothesis that not only do museums have national navels but that any museum can turn into an arena, a battlefield where political forces with distinctive national ideologies struggle to worm through potentially any subject, from art to architecture, archaeology, history, and so on. That's how science, in the Istanbul Museum of the History of Science and Technology in Islam, becomes national science, a tool in the hands of politicians who use it as an extension of their nationalist agenda. The same is true for Hungary, when Fidesz's government appointed a new director, György Fekete, to the Kunsthalle, an art museum. One of the most progressive art galleries in Europe, the Kunsthalle under Fekete began to exhibit art that mirrored the conservative views of the ruling party. A history museum, the House of the Hungarian Millennium, became a vitrine for Fidesz's national ideology and the much-debated Liget Project, the restructuring of Városliget Park in Budapest. In the House of Terror Museum, which exhibits predominantly on communist crimes in Hungary, Fidesz scores against the socialist opposition. In this museum, history functioned as the servant of nationalist politics. It would be possible to continue and present more evidence about the power of elites to impose specific national ideologies over the museum, but the result wouldn't change.

What is important is to acknowledge that these dynamics occur on top of an already existing structural normalisation and naturalisation of nationalism. Ideological clashes such as the ones mentioned previously, and with which this book is filled, occur only at the superstructural level, entirely within nationalism, which is hardly ever questioned. They are the product of nationalism as *natura naturans*, structure reproducing structure. That said, nationalism as a structural regularity in social life has by far the biggest impact on the museum as it makes it unquestioned and invisible to most. This doesn't mean that the analysis of these clashes is unimportant. On the contrary, they might shed light on attempts by agents to affect the structure and 'make history' (Sahlins, 1983 and 2005) in the sense of performing a shift in structural traditions that have their roots in the longue durée. Indeed, their results can tell us much about the spectrum of nationalism within the museum, which ranges theoretically from serving nationalism "above all" to not serving it "at all".

The problems posed by the first option are most evident when considering, for example, museums whose exhibits involve human rights violations. I refer to war museums, for example, the Kabatepe Simulation Center and Museum (Chapter 4); Holocaust museums, for example, the Holocaust Documentation Center in Budapest (Chapter 3); genocide, for example, the Jasenovac Memorial Museum (Chapter 5); and history museums, for example, the House of Terror Museum (Chapter 3). The core issue here is that to comply with nationalism, which demands not casting a shadow on the nation, to glorify it, commemorate it, and so on, the museum might resort to manipulation of the available evidence and even negationism and denialism. This occurs more often than one may think. To quote a few among the case studies of this book, the Kabatepe Simulation Center and Museum, the Panorama Museum 1453, and the Istanbul Museum of the History of Science and Technology in Islam (Chapter 4) all fall within this category. They do not exhibit real artefacts but reproductions that are combined in a way to build positive representations where national narratives are celebrated. At the same time, information that casts a shadow on the nation is concealed. As the case of the House of Terror Museum (Chapter 3) suggests, historical manipulation might also involve calibrating the visibility of historical evidence that might go against the ideology of the commissioner. Commissioned by national conservative Fidesz, this museum devotes 80% of the exhibit to the crimes of communism, against which Fidesz launched a real crusade, while only 20% is dedicated to the crimes of fascism.

Unlike museums in fully authoritarian regimes (e.g., Nazi Germany or fascist Italy), exhibiting nationalism in democracies (or aspiring ones) involves more subtle negotiations to avoid clashes with the principle of "Moral Remembrance", as Lea David calls the 'standards for a "proper" way of remembrance' (David, 2020: 1). At the core of these standards is the respect of human rights. As a matter of facts, the increasing organisational and ideological power that human rights ideology gained over the last decades reached museums worldwide through organisations such as the International Council of the Museums (ICOM) and its supporters, for example, the UN and UNESCO. The set of ICOM's postulates and axioms with which I began this book provides the museum with the ideological tools to render it more democratic, inclusive, polyphonic and less subject to narrow national interests. At the same time, international organisations devoted to heritage and memory such as UNESCO watch over irregularities and attempt to make their voice heard. This inevitably provokes clashes with the principle of state sovereignty that enables nationalist governments such as Hungary's or Turkey's to promote their own memorialisation agenda and rejects any interference from the outside. It is a phenomenon that reflects the competition between different although not necessarily incompatible ideologies: one that tends to put the nation and national interests above all, including advocates for democracy, inclusivity, and human rights.

That said, nationalism is a powerful ideology but it's not the only force affecting the museum. Globalisation, in particular the continuous global flow of people that is one of its main characteristics, has an impact on the museum. Its design and content requires it to adapt to increasingly wider audiences with specific needs and expectations. In addition, globalisation contributed to interconnectedness that in turn led to an increasing number of people who share the feeling of cosmopolitanism and thus feel more as members of a single community whose citizens are citizens of the world. This brings them to dismiss ethnic, cultural and/or religious backgrounds. It is inevitable that these dynamics affect the power of nationalism over museums. After all, the reason that pushed the Image of War Museum to represent the war beyond nationalism was the idea of fundamental equality between the parties, which were seen above all as part of one humanity and only after as Serbs and Croats.

The reality is that museums might be, and often are, the local extensions of ideological wars fought on a wider international scale. Whether and how national narratives in museums are affected by opposite forces such as nationalism and cosmopolitanism is still a matter of research. Some studies, including Mason (2013), Sassatelli (2018), Macdonald et al. (2017), Davidson and Pérez-Castellanos (2019), and others have already started to provide some insights. What these studies certainly prove is that the forces at the basis of cosmopolitanism are much stronger and visible in the present than, say, twenty years ago. The clashes that originate start to attract the attention of scholars of the museum and museum experts. From this perspective, museums might serve as local markers of changes that occur at the political and societal level, bringing evidence of the increasing organisational and ideological power of cosmopolitanism in modern society.

Museums that espouse the principles of inclusivity, democracy, and human rights tend to deflate nationalism, blocking it from worming its way through their representations and leaving it in the background. With the advance of moral remembrance, more and more museums embrace this modus operandi. What is interesting when scrutinising these phenomena closely is that they open a window into the precise moment when agency attempts to change a firmly established structure, proving that this is possible, although it might require sacrifices. The Image of War Museum in Zagreb (Chapter 5) and the Holocaust Documentation Center in Budapest (HDKE) (Chapter 3) are two of these museums. In the case of the HDKE, it exhibits strong evidence of Hungary's active role in the Holocaust, which is also the reason why it clashed with Fidesz's ruling government. However, the museum maintained internal autonomy and the exhibit wasn't subject to significant changes. It keeps working to revive the memory of the Holocaust in a way that is not influenced by ideology and political affiliation. In response, Fidesz's government announced the opening of another museum of the Holocaust, the House of Fate, which would substitute for the HDKE, now facing the dilemma of becoming a secondary choice, or worse, shut down. More clashes erupted, this time between part of the Jewish community of Budapest and the government against the building of this new museum that slowed down its construction. The museum is still not open at the time of this writing. Leaving details to the dedicated chapter, this case study suggests that nationalism's road to the museum might not be necessarily downhill, even for those who, like Fidesz, benefit from significant resources. This is particularly true when agents devoted to keeping nationalism out of the museum struggle to do so and are ready to sacrifice their job or even their personal safety.

In other cases, conditions are more favourable for museums whose goal is to exhibit beyond nationalism. Such is the case of the Image of War Museum (Chapter 5), a museum that focuses on the 1991–1995 war in Croatia between Croatian independentists and the Serb-led Yugoslav army. This museum found itself in an almost ideal scenario; being a private museum, self-funded, that wasn't subject to influence from the outside nor did it serve a specific political agenda. However, what this case study suggests is that favourable conditions do not always lead to success. Without getting into the details, which can be found in the dedicated chapter, it will suffice to say that this museum attempts to—but nonetheless partially fails to—represent the war beyond nationalism. When looking for an answer to this result given apparently ideal conditions, one risks blaming those who designed the museum, such as the curator, who in fact blames herself for not having been radical enough. However, following this logic would only provide a tautological and not an entirely correct answer to the reason for this failure. Even when scrutinising the curator's choices closely, one wouldn't necessarily find the reasons why the curator made them. The curator might not even know them. Instead, investigating the museum as the product of an interplay between structure and agency provides a track for identifying reasons that go beyond the individual curatorial process, the architectural process, and so on. This framework through which I attempted to analyse the museum is based on the fact that choices aren't made in a vacuum; neither are they free from structural pressures that might not be evident at first but influence them greatly. The reader will decide whether the results of this work were worth the effort that the author made to collect evidence of both structural and subjective elements influencing the museum.

With regards to the Image of War Museum, what following this track suggests is that nationalism dominates the representations of the 1991–1995 war in Croatia. This domination, redundant in many exhibits in Croatia, sets standards and models to follow. Standards and models represent an already established reality, a safe place as Nussbaum put it, equivalent to the 'comfort of local truths, the warm nestling feeling of nationalism, the absorbing drama of pride in oneself and one's own' (Nussbaum, 1996: 15). To go beyond it implies departing from certainty, going out of one's comfort zone, and entering unknown territory. This passage from certitude to incertitude inevitably entails several problems, including fear. Fear was the element that led the Image of War Museum to partially conform to other museums exhibiting on the 1991–1995 war. The Image of War Museum, and other museums in which nationalism dominates, might be seen as the victims of convention. They are the objectified representation of the domination of nationalism, its pressures and inducements. They are the projection of the oppressed that accumulated a long tradition of oppression and reproduce themselves in the form of business as usual. This model is so pervasive and invisible that, as this case study suggests, the curator ends up blaming herself for a failure that is not entirely attributable to her and her alone. It's not uncommon though.

The natural seeping of nationalism through the words of most of my interviewees—even the seemingly innocent identification with one group, which is evident in their use of expressions such as "us" and "them", Serbs and Croats, Turks and Kurds, Greeks and Turks, etc.—suggests that, although in varying degrees, nationalism is part of them, incarnated in them as embodied structure: nationalism in flesh and bones. One doesn't necessarily need to be aware of being a nationalist to act as one. This is important when coming to the museum, an institution that, as ICOM put it, is inclusive, polyphonic, and especially not for profit. Indeed, nationalism worms its way through the museum as much as it does through the people who work in or make museums. It is not the violent nationalism of swastikas and fasces but an everyday nationalism that is calm, subliminal, and unquestioned, and therefore, most powerful and undetected.

Note

1 I am simplifying here to make the text more readable. For an exact account of the Warwick Debate please read Nations and Nationalism's special issue on the Warwick Debates: '*The Nation: real or imagined? The Warwick Debates of Nationalism*. In Nations and Nationalism, Volume 2, Issue 3, Pages: 357–481. November 1996'.

Bibliography

Ahmad, F. (2008) The Late Ottoman Empire. In Kent, M. (ed.), *The Great Powers and the End of the Ottoman Empire*. Frank Cass, London. Pp. 5–31.

Ahmad, F. (2004) *The Making of Modern Turkey*. Routledge, London and New York.

Ahmad, F. (1984) The Late Ottoman Empire. In Kent M. (ed.) *The Great Powers and the End of the Ottoman Empire*. Frank Cass, London.

Aktar, A. (2000) Varlik Vergisi ve 'T0rkle4tirme' Politikalari [The Wealth Tax and the 'Turkification' Policies]. Iletisim. Istanbul. In Cagaptay, S. (2004) *Race, Assimilation and Kemalism: Turkish Nationalism and the Minorities in the 1930s. Middle Eastern Studies*. Vol. 40. No. 3. Pp. 86–101.

Akyol, M. (2014) Turkey's Rapid Museum Expansion. *Al-Monitor*. www.al-monitor.com/pulse/originals/2014/07/akyol-museum-rise-turkey-orhan-pamuk-culture-ministry.html (Last accessed 04/07/2018).

Alofsin, A. (2006) *When Buildings Speak: Architecture as Language in the Habsburg Empire and Its Aftermath*. University of Chicago Press, Chicago.

Althusser, L. (2001) *Lenin and Philosophy and Other Essays*, translated by B. Brewster. Monthly Review Press, New York, USA.

Anderson, B. (1991) *Imagined Communities: Reflections on the Origin and Spread of Nationalism*, Revised edition. Verso, London.

Apor, P. (2014) *Fabricating Authenticity in Soviet Hungary: The Afterlife of the First Hungarian Soviet Republic in the Age of State Socialism*. Anthem Press, London, UK.

Apor, P. (2012) Museum Policies in Hungary 1990–2010. In Eilertsen, Lill and Amundsen, Arne Bugge (eds.) *Museum Policies in Europe 1990–2010: Negotiating Professional and Political Utopia*. EuNaMus Report No 3. http://liu.diva-portal.org/smash/get/diva2:557284/FULLTEXT01 (Last accessed 11/04/2021).

Apor, P. (2011) *National Museums of Hungary*. In Aronnson, P. and Elgenius, G. (2011) *Building National Museums in Europe 1750–2010*. Conference proceedings from EuNaMus, European National Museums: Identity Politics, the Uses of the Past and the European Citizen, Bologna 28–30 April 2011. Peter Aronsson & Gabriella Elgenius (eds.) EuNaMus Report No 1. Published by Linköping University Electronic Press. www.ep.liu.se/ecp_home/index.en.aspx?issue=064

Aronsson, P. and Elgenius, G. (2015) *National Museums and Nation-Building in Europe 1750–2010, Mobilization and Legitimacy, Continuity and Change*. Routledge, London and New York.

Aronsson, P. and Elgenius, G. (2011) *Making National Museums in Europe: A Comparative Approach.* Conference Proceedings from EuNaMus, European National Museums: Identity, Politics, the Uses of the Past and the European Citizen, Bologna 28–30 April.

Ashplant, T. G., Dawson, G. and Roper, M. (2015) *The Politics of War Memory and Commemoration.* Routledge, London and New York.

Baab, J., Manheim, J. B., Rich, R. C., Willnat, L. and Brians, C. L. (2012) *Empirical Political Analysis: An Introduction to Research Methods.* Longman Publishing Group, London.

Baár, M. (2010) *Historians and Nationalism: East-Central Europe in the Nineteenth Century.* Oxford University Press, Oxford.

Bajomi, I., Bozóki, A., Csáki, J., Enyedi, Z., Fábián, I., Gábor, G., Gács, A., Galicza, P., Gyáni, G., Haris, A., Heller, M., Jászay, T., Kenesei, I., Klaniczay, G., Krusovszky, D., Kubínyi, K., Kulcsár, V., Lővei, P., Máté, A., Mélyi, J., Nagy, G., Pásztor, E., Polyák, G., Radó, P., Rényi, Á., Rényi, A., Sirató, I., Tőkei, É., Váradi, A. and Vásárhelyi, M. (2020) *Hungary Turns Its Back on Europe Dismantling Culture, Education, Science and the Media in Hungary 2010–2019.* Humán Platform. Oktatói Hálózat Hungarian Network of Academics, Budapest.

Bali, Rifat N. (1999) Cumhuriyet Yillarinda Tiirkiye Yahudileri: Bir Tiirkles, Tirme Seriiveni (1923–1945). Iletisim. Istanbul. In Cagaptay, S. (2004) *Race, Assimilation and Kemalism: Turkish Nationalism and the Minorities in the 1930s. Middle Eastern Studies.* Vol. 40. No. 3. Pp. 86–101.

Bektas, Y. and Sherman, R. (2013) A Bold New Enterprise: The Istanbul Museum of the History of Science and Technology in Islam. *Technology and Culture.* Vol. 54. No. 3. July. Pp. 619–639.

Belk, R. W. (1995) *Collecting in a Consumer Society.* Routledge, London.

Benčić, A. (2018) *Koncentracijski logor Jasenovac: konfliktno ratno nasljeđe i osporavani muzejski postav.* Polemos: časopis Za Interdisciplinarna Istraživanja. Rata, I Mira. P. 45.

Bennett, T. (2015a) Museums, Nations, Empires, Religions. In Aronsson, P. and Elgenius, G. (eds.) *National Museums and Nation-Building in Europe 1750–2010: Mobilization and Legitimacy, Continuity and Change.* Routledge, London and New York.

Bennett, T. (2015b) Thinking (with) Museums: From Exhibitionary Complex to Governmental Assemblage. In Macdonald, S. and Leahy, H. R. (eds.) *The International Handbooks of Museum Studies.* Wiley-Blackwell, Hoboken and New Jersey.

Bennett, T. (2004) The Exhibitionary Complex. In Preziosi, D. and Farago, C. (eds.) *Grasping the World: The Idea of the Museum* (Histories of Vision). Routledge, London and New York.

Bennett, T. (1995) *The Birth of the Museum, History, Theory, Politics.* Routledge, London and New York.

Billig, M. (1995) *Banal Nationalism.* Sage, London.

Blutinger, J. (2010) An Inconvenient Past: Post-Communist Holocaust Memorialization. *Purdue University Press.* Vol. 29. No. 1. Pp. 73–94.

Bonifačić, V. (1996) *Ethnological Research in Croatia.* Pregledni članak UDK 39(091)(497.5) 1919/1940 Primljeno: 22.10.1996. Nar, umjet. 33/2, 1996, str.

239–263, V. https://pdfs.semanticscholar.org/0f18/308e8fc03bb6b775e72829cf6 02f85637aed.pdf (Last accessed 09/09/2020).

Boswell, D. and Evans, J. (1999) *Representing the Nation: A Reader: Histories, Heritage, Museums*. Routledge, London and New York.

Bounia, A. and Stylianou-Lambert, T. L. (2011) *National Museums in Cyprus: A Story of Heritage and Conflict, in Building National Museums in Europe 1750–2010.* Conference proceedings from EuNaMus; European National Museums: Identity Politics; the Uses of the Past and the European Citizen; Bologna 28–30 April. EuNaMus Report No. 1.

Bourdieu, P. (2014) *Sur l'état*. Seuil, Paris, France.

Bourdieu, P. (1993) *The Field of Cultural Production*. Cambridge University Press, Cambridge.

Bourdieu, P. (1984) *Distinction: A Social Critique of the Judgement of Taste*. Harvard University Press, Cambridge, MA.

Bourdieu, P. and Chartier, R. (2015) *The Sociologist and the Historian*. Polity Press, Cambridge, UK.

Bourdieu, P. and Darbel, P. (1991) *The Love of Art: European Art Museums and Their Public*. Stanford University Press, Redwood City, California.

Bourdieu, P. and Wacquant, L. (1992) *An Invitation to Reflexive Sociology*. University of Chicago Press, Chicago.

Bozkuş, B. (2014) Rethinking Nationalism in the Case of 1453 Conquest Museum in Istanbul. *Global Media Journal: TR Edition*. Vol. 4. No. 8. Spring.

Bozoğlu, G. (2020) *Museums, Emotion, and Memory Culture: The Politics of the Past in Turkey*, 1st edition. Routledge, London and New York.

Brait, A. (2015) *(Dis)Embedding: The Institutionalization of the Social Memory of Totalitarian Pasts*. History of Communism in Europe. Vol. 6. Pp. 135–162.

Brandow-Faller, M. (2011) Art Nuveau and Hungarian Cultural Nationalism. In De Zepetnek, S. T. and Vasvári, L. O. (eds.) *Comparative Hungarian Cultural Studies*. Purdue University Press, West Lafayette, Indiana, USA.

Breuilly, J. (1982) *Nationalism and the State*. University of Chicago Press, Chicago, US.

Brubaker, R. (2017) *Grounds for Difference*. Harvard University Press, Cambridge.

Brubaker, R. (2015) *Grounds for Difference*. Harvard University Press, Cambridge.

Brubaker, R. (1992) *Nationalism Reframed, Nationhood and the National Question in the New Europe*. Cambridge University Press, Cambridge.

Cagaptay, S. (2017) *The New Sultan: Erdogan and the Crisis of Modern Turkey*. I.B. Tauris Press, London and New York.

Calhoun, C. (1997) *Nationalism*. University of Minnesota Press, Minneapolis.

Catalogue of the Military Museum (2015) *Harbiye Askeri Müzesi*. Kristal Reklam Baskı, Istanbul.

Chrzová, B. (2018) 'Long Live the Serbian Nation!': The Republika Srpska Commemoration of Jasenovac Victims. *Primus Bohems Web*, 27.4. www.bohems.fsv.cuni.cz/post/91 (Last accessed 24/02/2021).

Constitution of the Republic of Croatia (2010) https://www.constituteproject.org/constitution/Croatia_2010.pdf?lang=en (Last accessed 26/09/2021).

Croatia News (2019) *Zagreb 80s Museum Officially Opens in Heart of Shanghai*, 27.11. www.total-croatia-news.com/lifestyle/39862-zagreb-80s-museum (Last accessed 08/03/2021).

Crooke, E. (2007) *Museums and Community: Ideas, Issues and Challenges*. Routledge, London and New York.

Crow, J. (2009) Narrating the Nation: Chile's Museo Histórico Nacional. *National Identities*. Vol. 11. No. 2.

Csipke, Z. (2011) The Changing Significance of the 1956 Revolution in Post-Communist Hungary. *Europe-Asia Studies*. Vol. 63. No. 1. Pp. 99–18. In Webb, H. (year unknown) Political Conflict in Contemporary Hungary Expressed through Competing Collective Memories of the 1956 Hungarian Revolution. Published on Academia.edu. www.academia.edu/14789374/Political_Conflict_in_Contemporary_Hungary_expressed_through_Competing_Collective_Memories_of_the_1956_Hungarian_Revolution (Last accessed 14/04/2021).

David, L. (2020) *The Past Can't Heal Us: The Dangers of Mandating Memory in the Name of Human Rights*. Cambridge University Press, Cambridge.

Davidson, L. and Pérez-Castellanos, L. (2019) *Cosmopolitan Ambassadors: International Exhibitions, Cultural Diplomacy and the Polycentral Museum*. Vernon Press, Delawer, USA.

Dulibić, L. and Pasini Tržec, I. (2016) The Strossmayer Gallery in Zagreb in the Interwar Period: From a Utopian Project to a Renowned Institution. *Il Capitale Culturale*. Vol. 14. Pp. 613–634. ISSN 2039–2362. http://dx.doi.org/10.13138/2039-2362/1393

Duncan, C. (2013) Rituals in the Early Louvre Museum. In Tsang, R. (ed.) *The Cultural Politics of Nationalism and Nation-Building: Ritual and Performance in the Forging of Nations*. Routledge, London and New York.

Duncan, C. (1995) *Civilizing Rituals: Inside Public Art Museums*. Routledge, London and New York.

Duncan, C. and Wallach, A. (1980) The Universal Survey Museum. *Art History*. Vol. 3. No. 4. Pp. 448–469.

Echikson, W. (2019) *Holocaust Remembrance Project*. https://docs.wixstatic.com/ugd/c1aa54_d6fdacf05b6845a3a2cacbf80ed6720c.pdf (Last accessed 09/03/2021).

The Economist (2016) A War to Remember: Turkey's Shallow Ottomania. www.economist.com/blogs/prospero/2016/08/war-remember

Elgenius, G. (2015) National Museums as National Symbols: A Survey of Strategic Nation-building and Identity Politics: Nations as Symbolic Regimes. In Aronsson, P. and Elgenius, G. (eds.) *National Museums and Nation-Building in Europe 1750–2010, Mobilization and Legitimacy, Continuity and Change*. Routledge, Abingdon, UK.

Eligür, B. (2010) *The Mobilization of Political Islam in Turkey*. Cambridge University Press, Cambridge.

Eriksen, T. H. (2007) Nationalism and the Internet. *Nations and Nationalism*. Vol. 13. No. 1. Pp. 1–17.

Foucault, M. (1991) Governmentality. In Burchell, G., Gordon, C. and Miller, P. (eds.) *The Foucault Effect*. Wheatsheaf Harvester, London.

Foucault, M. (1975) *Surveiller et punir*. Gallimard, Paris.

Foucault, M. (1966) *Les mots et les choses—une archéologie des sciences humaines*. Gallimard, Paris.

Fox. J. (2018) Banal Nationalism in Everyday Life. *Nations and Nationalism*. Vol. 24. No. 4. Pp. 862–866.

Fox, J. and Miller-Idriss, C. (2008) Everyday Nationhood. *Ethnicities, SAGE Publications*. Vol. 8. No. 4. Pp. 536–563.

Frigyesi, J. (1994) Béla Bartók and the Concept of Nation and 'Volk' in Modern Hungary. *The Musical Quarterly*. Vol. 78. No. 2. Summer. Pp. 255–287.

Fyfe, G. (2011) Sociology and the Social Aspects of Museums In Macdonald, S. (ed.) *A Companion to Museum Studies*. Wiley Blackwell, Hoboken and New Jersey, USA. Pp. 33–49.

Gellner, E. (1983) *Nations and Nationalism*. Cornell University Press, Ithaca, NY.

Goldstein, I. and Goldstein, S. (2016) [First edition in Serbo-Croatian in 2001] *The Holocaust in Croatia*. University of Pittsburgh Press in Association with the United States Holocaust Memorial Museum, Pittsburgh.

Goodwin, J. and Horowitz, R. (2002) Introduction: The Methodological Strengths and Dilemmas of Qualitative Sociology. *Qualitative Sociology*. Vol. 25. No. 1. Pp. 172–194.

Guibernau, M. (2003) Nationalism and Intellectuals in Nations without States: The Catalan Case. *WP núm*. 222. Institut de Ciències Polítiques i Socials. www.icps.cat/archivos/WorkingPapers/wp222.pdf?noga=1

Gümüşçü, Ş. and Sert, D. (2009) The Power of the Devout Bourgeoisie: The Case of the Justice and Development Party in Turkey. *Middle Eastern Studies*. Vol. 45. No. 6. Pp. 953–968.

Gyani, G. (2008) Memory and Discourse on the 1956 Hungarian Revolution. In Cox, T. (ed.) *Challenging Communism in Eastern Europe: 1956 and Its Legacy*. Routledge, New York.

Hadas, M. (2007) Gymnastic Exercises or 'Work Wrapped in the Gown of Youthful Joy': Masculities and the Civilizing Process in 19th Century Hungary. *Journal of Social History*. Vol. 41, No. 1. Oxford University Press, Oxford. Pp. 161–180.

Hall, J. and Malešević, S. (2013) *Nationalism and War*. Cambridge University Press, Cambridge.

Harvey, W. S. (2009) *Methodological Approaches for Junior Researchers Interviewing Elites: A Multidisciplinary Perspective*. Economic Geography Research Group Working Paper Series No. 01.09. www.egrg.rgs.org/wp-content/uploads/2014/02/egrg_wp0109-Harvey.pdf (Last accessed 10/04/2021).

Hirschberger, G. (2018) Collective Trauma and the Social Construction of Meaning. *Frontiers of Psychology*. www.frontiersin.org/articles/10.3389/fpsyg.2018.01441/full (Last accessed 14/04/2021).

Hobsbawm, E. and Ranger, T. (eds.) (1983) *The Invention of Tradition*. Cambridge University Press, Cambridge.

Hofer, T. (1990) Construction of the 'Folk Cultural Heritage' in Hungary and Rival Versions of National Identity. *Ethnologia Europaea*. Vol. 21. No. 1. https://doi.org/10.16995/ee.1291

Hooper-Greenhill, E. (1992) *Museums and the Shaping of Knowledge*. Routledge, London and New York.

Human Rights Watch (2016) *Turkey: Academics Jailed For Signing Petition Hundreds Investigated for 'Terrorism'*. www.hrw.org/news/2016/03/16/turkey-academics-jailed-signing-petition (Last accessed 14/04/2021).

Hürriyet Daily News (2014) *Erdoğan Vows to Teach Turkish Children Muslim Discovery of Americas*. www.hurriyetdailynews.com/erdogan-vows-to-teach-turkish-children-muslim-discovery-of-americas-74485 (Last accessed 14/04/2021).

Hutchison, E. (2016) *Affective Communities in World Politics, Collective Emotions after Trauma*. Cambridge University Press, Cambridge.

ICOM (2019) *Museum Definition; Creating a New Museum Definition: The Backbone of ICOM*. https://icom.museum/en/activities/standards-guidelines/museum-definition/ (Accessed 30/09/2019).

Jenne, E. K. (2018) Is Nationalism or Ethnopopulism on the Rise Today? *Ethnopolitics*. Vol. 17. No. 5. P. 549.

Jonášová, M. (2019) Hungarian art in the age of Viktor Orbán. *ArtPortal Published*, 06/11. https://artportal.hu/magazin/hungarian-art-in-the-age-of-viktor-orban/ (Last accessed 11/04/2021).

Jung, M. K. (2015) Symbolic and Physical Violence: Legitimate State Coercion of Filipino Workers in Prewar Hawaii. *American Studies*. Vol. 45. No. 3. Fall. Pp. 107–137.

Jungwatanawong, I. (2014) *Historical Memory as a Political Tool for Legitimacy by FIDESZ Government in Hungary*. M.A. Thesis. Lund University. file:///C:/Users/loren/Downloads/Historical_Memory_as_a_Political_Tool_fo.pdf

Király, B. (2001) *Basic History of Modern Hungary, 1867–1999*. Krieger, Florida, USA.

Knell, S. J. (2011) National Museums and the National Imagination. In Knell, S. J., Aronsson, P. and Amudsen, A. B. (eds.) *National Museums: New Studies from around the World*. Routledge, London and New York.

Kolstø, P. (2011) The Serbian-Croatian Controversy over Jasenovac. In Ramet, S. P. and Listhaug, O. (eds.) *Serbia and the Serbs in World War Two*. Palgrave MacMillan, London, UK. Pp. 225–246.

Kühn, T. (2007) Shaping and Reshaping Colonial Ottomanism: Contesting Boundaries of Difference and Integration in Ottoman Yemen. *Comparative Studies of South Asia, Africa and the Middle East*. Vol. 27. No. 2. Pp. 315–331.

Kurimay, A. (2016) Interrogating the Historical Revisionism of the Hungarian Right: The Queer Case of Cécile Tormay. *East European Politics and Societies and Cultures*. Vol. 30. No. 1. February. Pp. 10–33.

Lajosi, K. (2018) *Staging the Nation: Opera and Nationalism in 19th-Century Hungary*. Brill, Leiden, Netherlands.

Liget Project (2021) *Liget Budapest Project*. https://ligetbudapest.hu/en/liget-budapest-project (Last accessed 14/04/2021).

Liu, Y. and Zhou, S. (2019) *Evolving Chinese Nationalism: Using the 2015 Military Parade as a Case*. In East Asia. Vol. 36. I. 3. Springer, New York.

Lukic, N. G. (2011) National Museums in Croatia. In Aronsson, P. and Elgenius, G. (eds.) *Building National Museums in Europe 1750–2010*. Conference proceedings from EuNaMus, European National Museums: Identity Politics, the Uses of the Past and the European Citizen, Bologna 28–30 April 2011. EuNaMus Report No 1. Published by Linköping University Electronic Press. www.ep.liu.se/ecp_home/index.en.aspx?issue=064

Macdonald, S. (ed.) (2011) *A Companion to Museum Studies*. Wiley Blackwell, Hoboken and New Jersey.

Macdonald, S. (2003) Museums, National, Postnational and Transcultural Identities. *Museum and Society*. Vol. 1. No. 1. Pp. 1–16.

Macdonald, S., Lidchi, H. and Von Oswald, M. (2017) Engaging Anthropological Legacies toward Cosmo-Optimistic Futures? *Museum Worlds: Advances in Research*. Vol. 5. Pp. 95–107.

Makdisi, U. (2002) Rethinking Ottoman Imperialism: Modernity, Violence and the Cultural Logic of Ottoman Reform. In Hanssen, J., Philip, T. and Weber, S. (eds.) *The Empire in the City: Arab Provincial Capitals in the Late Ottoman Empire*. Orient-Institut, Beirut.

Malešević, S. (2019) *Grounded Nationalisms: A Sociological Analysis*. Cambridge University Press, Cambridge, UK.

Malešević, S. (2017). *The rise of organised brutality: A historical sociology of violence*. Cambridge, Cambridge University Press.

Malešević, S. (2013a) *Nation-States and Nationalisms: Organizations, Ideology, Solidarity*. Polity Press, Cambridge.

Malešević, S. (2013b) Is Nationalism Intrinsically Violent? *Nationalism and Ethnic Politics*. Vol. 19. No. 1. Pp. 12–37.

Malešević, S. (2012a) Wars That Make States and Wars That Make Nations: Prganised Violence, Nationalism and State Formation in the Balkans. *European Journal of Sociology*. Vol. 53. No. 1. Pp. 31–63.

Malešević, S. (2012b) Did Wars Make Nation-States in the Balkans?: Nationalisms, Wars and States in the 19th and Early 20th Century South East Europe. *Journal of Historical Sociology*. Vol. 25. No. 3. Pp. 299–330.

Malešević, S. (2010) *The Sociology of War and Violence*. Cambridge University Press, Cambridge.

Malešević, S. (2002) *Ideology, Legitimacy and the New State: Yugoslavia, Serbia and Croatia*. Routledge, London and New York.

Manchin, A. (2015) Staging Traumatic Memory: Competing Narratives of State Violence in Post-Communist Hungarian Museums. *East European Jewish Affairs*. Vol. 45. No. 2–3. Pp. 236–251.

Mann, M. (1995) *A Political Theory of Nationalism and Its Excesses*. Central European University Press, Budapest.

Mason, R. (2013) National Museums, Globalization, and Postnationalism: Imagining a Cosmopolitan Museology. *Museum Worlds: Advances in Research*. Vol. 1. No. 1. Pp. 40–64.

Mason, R., Robinson, A. and Coffield, E. (2018) *Museum and Galley Studies: The Basics*. Routledge, London and New York.

Marsovszky M. (2011) „Die Märtyrer sind die Magyaren“. In: Globisch C., Pufelska A., Weiß V. (eds) *Die Dynamik der europäischen Rechten. VS Verlag für Sozialwissenschaften*. https://doi.org/10.1007/978-3-531-92703-9_4

Mataušić, N. (2003) *Jasenovac 1941–1945: logor smrti i radni logor*. Javna ustanova Spomen-područje Jasenovac, Jasenovac-Zagreb.

Mclean, F. (2006) Introduction: Heritage and Identity. *International Journal of Heritage Studies*. Vol. 12. No. 1. Heritage and Identity.

Mclean, F. (2005) Museums and National Identity. *Museum and Society*. Vol. 3. No. 1. March. Pp. 1–4.

Megill, A. (1995) *Grand Narrative and the Discipline of History: A New Philosophy of History*, edited by Frank Ankersmit and Hans Kellner. University of Chicago Press, Chicago.

Meltzer, D. J. (1981) Ideological and Material Culture. In Gould, R. J. and Schiffer, M. B. (eds.) *Modern Material Culture: The Archaeology of Us*. Academic Press, New York. Pp. 113–125.

Military Museum and Cultural Center Command (2015) *Cyprus Peace Operation Exhibition at 41 St Anniversary*; Minstry of Culture and Tourism (2015) *Where the Hearth of a Nation Beasts: Gallipoli*. BüyükHarf Production, Printer Özel Matbaası Anakara.

Mills, C. W. (2000 [First edition in 1956]) *The Power Elite*. Oxford University Press, Oxford, USA.

Milošević, A. and Touquet, H. (2018) *Unintended Consequences: The EU Memory Framework and the Politics of Memory in Serbia and Croatia*. Southeast European and Black Sea Studies. Vol. 18. I. 3. Pp. 381–399.

Ministry of Forestry and Water (2012) *Gallipoli Peninsula National Park*. www.milliparklar.gov.tr/kitap/55/55.pdf

Molnar, G. (2007) Hungarian Football: A Socio-Historical Overview. *Sport in History*. Vol. 27. No. 2. Pp. 293–317.

Navaro Yashin, Y. (2009) Confinement and the Imagination: Sovereignty and Subjectivity in a Quasi-State. In Blom Hansen, T. and Stepputat, F. (eds.) *Sovereign Bodies: Citizens, Migrants, and States in the Postcolonial World*. Princeton University Press, Princeton, NJ. Pp. 103–119.

Newman, A. and McLean, F. (2006) The Impact of Museums upon Identity. *International Journal of Heritage Studies*. Vol. 12. No. 1. Heritage and Identity.

The New York Times (2016) Newspaper Closes in Hungary, and Hungarians See Government's Hand. ISSN 0362–4331 (Last accessed 07/06/2021).

Nolan, D. (2014) Budapest Kunsthalle to Emphasize Traditional over Contemporary Art. *The Budapest Beacon*. https://budapestbeacon.com/budapest-kunsthalle-to-emphasize-traditional-over-contemporary-art/ (Accessed 12/02/2021).

Nussbaum, M. C. (1996) Patriotism and Cosmopolitanism. In Cohen, Joshua (ed.) *For Love of Country*. Beacon Press, Boston.

Öncü, A. (2007) The Politics of Istanbul's Ottoman Heritage in the Era of Globalism: Refractions through the Prism of a Theme Park. In Drieskens, B., Mermier, F. and Wimmen, H. (eds.) *Cities of the South: Citizenship and Exclusion in the 21st Century*. Saqi Books, London, Beirut. Pp. 233–264.

Öncü, A. (1999) Istanbulites and Others: The Cultural Cosmology of Being Middle Class in the Era of Globalization. In Keyder, Ç. (ed.) *Istanbul: Between the Global and the Local*. Rowman and Littlefield, Lanham. Pp. 95–119.

Palabıyık M. S. (2016) The Sultan, the Shah and the King in Europe: The Practice of Ottoman, Persian and Siamese Royal Travel and Travel Writing. *Journal of Asian History*. Vol. 50, No. 2. Pp. 201–234.

Palhegyi, J. (2018) Revolutionary Curating, Curating the Revolution: Socialist Museology in Yugoslav Croatia. *Martor*. Vol. 23. Pp. 17–34. https://d1wqtxts1xzle7.cloudfront.net/57731846/Revolutionary_Curating__Curating_the_Revolution_Socialist_Museology_in_Yugoslav_Croatia_Palhegyi.pdf?1541821050=&response-content-disposition=inline%3B+filename%3DRevolutionary_Curating_Curating_the_Revo.pdf&Expires=1599657205&Signature=f9cl5CpFF31mDMEUqNN8a8857BprxNN64JK9u1srR-2sD-ZLmbdDVafxQuNqHwpo1C1UT06KoAjkEqvzGledMnxQca1PBiw54SNj93AUWOKuCbpzYP~P-1W85QF-3vh7-reXdAp189NUw59OOOWz-yorUmdnzCZDHxhAPC6G7heHrrzrSSjuJZF1SYBeLSYGT4ZIIW3pkWs3cXO30qu2GV4rLFa2xrAiPLLbMleDu1o00WwbKLc7Vgem3UOIVzUxNZK7byHb5a2jOJotuHZeAwHKTPxcsDlkBOQ9b74Z94wV3Vs1bW-bv-OLLUwYb9-6VjgHkyOSK9-HQ8xrDA__&Key-Pair-Id=APKAJLOHF5GGSLRBV4ZA (Last accessed 09/09/2020).

Palhegyi, J. (2017) National Museums, National Myths: Constructing Socialist Yugoslavism for Croatia and Croats. *Nationalities Papers*. Vol. 45. No. 6. Pp. 1048–1065.

Pérouse, J. F. and Cheviron, N. (2016) *Erdoğan: Nouveau père de la Turquie?* Editions François Bourin, Paris.

Pető, A. (2021) The Illiberal Memory Politics in Hungary. *Journal of Genocide Research*. DOI: 10.1080/14623528.2021.1968150

Pető, A. (2016) Revisionist Histories, 'Future Memories': Far-Right Memorialization Practices in Hungary. *European Politics and Society*. http://dx.doi.org/10.1080/23745118.2016.1269442

Poll, R. (2012) *Afterward: The Global Village*. Rutgers University Press. New Brunswick, New Jersey.

Posocco, L. (2020) The Politics of Nationalism in Recently Built Turkish Museums: The Case of the Kabatepe Simulation Centre and Museum. *International Journal of Politics Culture and Society*. Vol. 33. No. 1. Pp. 67–87.

Potkonjac, S. and Pletenac, T. (2016) *Post-Yugoslav Constellations: The Art and Craft of Memory: Re-Memorialization Practices in Post-Socialist Croatia*. De Gruyter, Berlin.

Pytlas, B. (2013) Radical-Right Narratives in Slovakia and Hungary: Historical Legacies, Mythic Overlaying and Contemporary Politics. *Patterns of Prejudice*. Vol. 47. No. 2.

Radonić, L. (2020) 'Our' vs. 'Inherited' Museums: PiS and Fidesz as Mnemonic Warriors. *Südosteuropa*. Vol. 68. No. 1. Pp. 44–78. https://doi.org/10.1515/soeu-2020-0003

Radonić, L. (2018) The Holocaust Template: Memorial Museums in Hungary, Croatia and Bosnia-Herzegovina. *Anali*. Vol. 15. No. 1. Pp. 131–154.

Radonić, L. (2017) Post-Communist Invocation of Europe: Memorial Museums' Narratives and the Europeanization of Memory. *National Identities*. Vol. 19. No. 2. Narrating European Integration: Transnational Actors and Stories.

Radonić, L. (2011) Croatia: Exhibiting Memory and History at the 'Shores of Europe'. *Culture Unbound*. Vol. 3. Pp. 355–367. Hosted by Linköping University Electronic Press. www.cultureunbound.ep.liu.se

Rivera, L. A. (2008) Managing 'Spoiled' National Identity: War, Tourism, and Memory in Croatia. *American Sociological Review*. Vol. 73. No. 4. Pp. 613–634.

Ross, D. (1995) Grand Narrative in American Historical Writing: From Romance to Uncertainty. *The American Historical Review*. Vol. 100. No. 3. June. Pp. 651–677.

Rushton, J. P. (2005) Ethnic Nationalism, Evolutionary Psychology and Genetic Similarity Theory. *Nations and Nationalism*. Vol. 11. No. 4. Pp. 489–507.

Saatçioğlu, B. (2010) *Unpacking the Compliance Puzzle: The Case of Turkey's AKP under EU Conditionality*. KFG Working Paper Series, No. 14, June 2010, Kolleg-Forschergruppe (KFG) *The Transformative Power of Europe*. Freie Universität Berlin.

Sahlins, M. (2005) Structural Work: How Microhistories Become Macrohistories and Vice Versa. *Anthropological Theory*. Vol. 5. No. 1. Pp. 5–30.

Sahlins, M. (1983) Other Times, Other Customs: The Anthropology of History. *Anthrosource*. Wiley. Hoboken, New Jersey. Vol. 85. I. 3. Pp. 517–544.

SAMA (1999) Sama's Definition of Museum. In Mason, R., Robinson, A. and Coffield, E. (eds.) (2018) *Museum and Galley Studies: The Basics*. Routledge, London and New York.

Sang-hoon, J. (2020) *A Representation of Nationhood in the Museum: The National Museum of Korea*. Routledge, London and New York.

Saraçoğlu, C. and Demirkol, Ö. (2015) Nationalism and Foreign Policy Discourse in Turkey Under the AKP Rule: Geography, History and National Identity. *British Journal of Middle Eastern Studies*. Vol. 42. No. 3. Pp. 301–319.

Sassatelli, S. (2018) Festivals, Museums, Exhibitions: Aesthetic Cosmopolitanism in the Cultural Public Sphere. In Delanty, G. (ed.) *Routledge International Handbook of Cosmopolitanism Studies*. Routledge, London and New York.

Scorrano, A. (2011) Constructing National Identity: National Representations at the Museum of Sydney. *Journal of Australian Studies*. Vol. 36. No. 3.

Shcherbak, A. (2015) *Nationalism in the USSR: A Historical and Comparative Perspective*. Higher School of Economics Research Paper No. WP BRP 27/SOC/2013. https://papers.ssrn.com/sol3/papers.cfm?abstract_id=2366789 (Last accessed 14/04/2021).

Ščukanec, D. (1957) *Od Partizahnskih Odreda do Jugoslavenske Armije* [From Partizan Unit to Yugoslav Army]. Museum of the Revolution of the Peoples of Croatia, Zagreb. Quoted in Palhegyi, J. (2018) Revolutionary Curating, Curating the Revolution: Socialist Museology in Yugoslav Croatia. *Martor*. Vol. 23. Pp. 17–34.

Shaw, W. M. K. (2011) *National Museums in the Republic of Turkey: Palimpsests within a Centralized State, in Building National Museums in Europe 1750–2010*. Conference proceedings from EuNaMus, European National Museums: Identity Politics, the Uses of the Past and the European Citizen, Bologna 28–30 April

2011. Peter Aronsson & Gabriella Elgenius (eds) EuNaMus Report No 1. Published by Linköping University Electronic Press. www.ep.liu.se/ecp_home/index.en.aspx?issue=064

Shaw, W. M. K. (2007) Museums and Narratives of Display from the Late Ottoman Empire to the Turkish Republic. *Muqarnas Online*. Vol. 24. No. 1. Pp. 253–279.

Shaw, W. M. K. (1999) *Possessors and Possessed, Museums, Archaeology, and the Visualization of History in the Late Ottoman Empire*. University of California Press, Berkley and Los Angeles, CA.

Shelton, A. (2013) Critical Museology: A Manifesto. *Museum Worlds: Advances in Research*. Vol. 1. No. 7. Pp. 7–23.

Skey, M. (2009) The National in Everyday Life: A Critical Engagement with Michael Billig's Thesis of Banal Nationalism. *The Sociological Review*. Vol. 57. No. 2. May. Pp. 331–346.

Skey, M. and Antonsich, M. (2017) *Everyday Nationhood: Theorising Culture, Identity and Belonging after Banal Nationalism*. Palgrave, London, UK.

Smith, A. D. (2009) *Ethnosymbolism and Nationalism*. A Cultural Approach, Routledge, UK.

Smith, A. D. (1996) Memory and Modernity: Reflections on Ernest Gellner's Theory of Nationalism. *Nations and Nationalism*. Vol. 2. No. 3. Pp. 371–388.

Smith, L. (2006) *Uses of Herigage*. Routledge, London and New York.

Sodaro, A. (2017) *Exhibiting Atrocity Book Subtitle: Memorial Museums and the Politics of Past Violence*. Rutgers University Press. New Brunswick, New Jersey.

SRGG (2017) *Authoritarianism before and after the 15 July 2016 Coup in Turkey*. http://regnet.anu.edu.au/news-events/news/7024/authoritarianism-and-after-15-july-2016-coup-turkey (Last accessed 14/04/2021).

Steinvorth, D. (2009) *Nostalgia for the Ottomans: Disillusioned with Europe, Turkey Looks East*. www.spiegel.de/international/world/nostalgia-for-the-ottomans-disillusioned-with-europe-turkey-looks-east-a-660635.html (Accessed 04/07/2018).

Taspinar, O. (2018) Turkey Takes a Big Step toward Nationalist Fascism. *The Washington Post*. www.washingtonpost.com/news/theworldpost/wp/2018/06/25/erdogan/ (Last accessed 14/04/2021).

The Fundamental Law of Hungary (2011) https://www.constituteproject.org/constitution/Hungary_2011.pdf (Last accessed 26/09/2021).

Thorpe, J. (2015) Exhibiting the Austro-Hungarian Empire: The Austrian Museum for Folk Culture in Vienna, 1895–1925. *Museum & Society*. Vol. 13. No. 1. Pp. 42–51.

Tilly, C. (1996) The State of Nationalism. *Critical Review*. Vol. 10. Pp. 299–306.

Tilly, C. (1994) States and Nationalism in Europe 1492–1992. *Theory and Society*. Springer. Vol. 23. No. 1. Pp. 131–146.

Tucker, S. C. (1996) *The European Powers in the First World War*. An Encyclopaedia. Garland Publishing, New York.

Tuğal, C. (2009) *Passive Revolution: Absorbing the Islamic Challenge to Capitalism*. Stanford University Press, Stanford.

Türeli, I. (2006) Modelling Citizenship in Turkey's Miniature Park. *Traditional Dwellings and Settlements Review*. Vol. 17. No. 2. Pp. 55–69.

Turkish Constitution (2017) http://Constituteproject.org/constitution/Turkey_2017.pdf?lang=en (Accessed 28/03/2020).

Uludağ, S. (2004) The Slow Burial of the Patterns of 'Nationalism'. *Αλήθεια*, 26.09. Also Uludağ, S. (2005) *Cyprus: The Untold Stories: A Reader*. Bibliopolis.

UNESCO (2020) *UNESCO Statement on Hagia Sophia, Istanbul*. https://en.unesco.org/news/unesco-statement-hagia-sophia-istanbul (Last accessed 06/04/2021).

USHMM (2016) *Museum Condemns Conferring of Hungarian Order of Merit to Zsolt Bayer*. www.ushmm.org/information/press/press-releases/museum-condemns-conferring-of-hungarian-order-of-merit-to-zsolt-bayer (Last accessed 14/04/2021).

Van Aalst, I. and Boogaarts, I. (2002) From Museum to Mass Entertainment, the Evolution of the Role of Museums in Cities. *European Urban and Regional Studies*. Vol. 9. No. 3. Pp. 195–209.

Van der Laarse, R. (2013) Beyond Auschwitz? Europe's Terrorscapes in the Age of Postmemory. In Silberman, M. and Vatan, F. (eds.) *Memory and Postwar Memorials Confronting the Violence of the Past*. Palgrave MacMillan, New York, USA.

Vásárhelyi, T. (2012) The Hungarian Patient: Museum Education in Hungary and the Challenges of Democratic Transition. *Journal of Museum Education*. Vol. 37. No. 3. Pp. 15–30.

Von Scheve, C. and Salmela, M. (2014) *Collective Emotions*. Oxford University Press, Oxford.

Vranić, I. (2016) Nationalization of material culture in the late 19th century Triune Kingdom of Croatia. In The ethnic and social: the forms of interplay and conflicts. Sankt-Peterburg, Russia. At https://www.bib.irb.hr/1052803 (Last accessed 26/09/2021).

Vukov, N. (2011) Conceptualizing Folklore along 'Disciplinary Lines': The Political Entanglement of Folklore Studies in Socialist Bulgaria. In Brunnbauer, U., Kraft, C., and Schulze Wessel, M. (eds.) *Sociology and Ethnography in East-Central and South-East Europe: Scientific Self-Description in State Socialist Countries*. Bad Wiesseer Tagungen des Collegium Carolinum, Bd. 31, Munich. Pp. 243–262.

Watson, S. Barnes, A. J. and Bunning, K. (2019) *A Museum Studies Approach to Heritage*. Routledge, London and New York.

Walton, J. and Göktürk, D. (2010) Practices of Neo-Ottomanism: Making Space and Place Virtuous in Istanbul. In Gokturk, D., Soysal, L. and Tureli, I. (eds.) *Orienting Istanbul, Cultural Capital of Europe*. Routledge, Abingdon, UK.

Watson, S. and Sawyer, A. (2011) *National Museums in Britain*. Building National Museums in Europe 1750–2010. Conference proceedings from EuNaMus, European National Museums: Identity Politics, the Uses of the Past and the European Citizen, Bologna 28–30 April 2011. Peter Aronsson & Gabriella Elgenius (eds) EuNaMus Report No 1. Published by Linköping University Electronic Press. www.ep.liu.se/ecp_home/index.en.aspx?issue=064 © The Author.

West, B. (2010) Dialogical Memorialization, International Travel and the Public Sphere: A Cultural Sociology of Commemoration and Tourism at the First World War Gallipoli Battlefields. *Tourist Studies*. Vol. 10. No. 3. Pp. 209–225.

White, J. (2009) *Muslim Nationalism and the New Turks.* Princeton University Press, Princeton, USA.

Wimmer, A. and Glick Schiller, N. (2003) Methodological Nationalism, the Social Sciences, and the Study of Migration: An Essay in Historical Epistemology. *The International Migration Review.* Vol. 37. No. 3. Transnational Migration: International Perspectives (Fall). Pp. 576–610 (35 pages).

Wright, F. (1988) Reconciling the Histories of Protestant and Catholic in Northern Ireland. In Falconer, Alan D. (ed.) *Reconciling Memories.* Columba Press, Dublin, Ireland.

Yeni Şafak (2014) *Muslims Discovered America!* www.yenisafak.com/en/life/muslims-discovered-america!-2026697 (Last accessed 14/04/2021).

Yennaris, C. (2003) *From the East: Conflict and Partition in Cyprus*, 1st edition. Elliot & Thompson Ltd, London, UK.

Yilmaz, A. (2014) Memorialization on War-Broken Ground: Gallipoli War Cemeteries and Memorials Designed by Sir John James Burnet. *Journal of the Society of Architectural Historians.* Vol. 73. No. 3. Pp. 328–346.

Žižek, S. (1994) The Spectre of Ideology. In Žižek, S. (ed.) *Mapping Ideology.* Verso, London and New York.

Žižek, S. (1989) *The Sublime Object of Ideology.* Verso, London and New York.

Żychlińska, M. and Fontana, E. (2016) Museal Games and Emotional Truths Creating Polish National Identity at the Warsaw Rising Museum. *East European Politics and Society.* Sage. Vol. 30. No. 2.

Index

Note: Page numbers in *italics* indicate a figure on the corresponding page.

For Product Safety Concerns and Information please contact our EU representative GPSR@taylorandfrancis.com
Taylor & Francis Verlag GmbH, Kaufingerstraße 24, 80331 München, Germany

www.ingramcontent.com/pod-product-compliance
Lightning Source LLC
LaVergne TN
LVHW020640100826
845148LV00012B/2255

* 9 7 8 0 3 6 7 5 1 2 4 8 4 *